A POLITICAL PHILOSOPHY IN PUBLIC LIFE

A POLITICAL PHILOSOPHY IN PUBLIC LIFE

CIVIC REPUBLICANISM IN ZAPATERO'S SPAIN

JOSÉ LUIS MARTÍ
AND
PHILIP PETTIT

PRINCETON UNIVERSITY PRESS   PRINCETON AND OXFORD

Published by Princeton University Press, 41 William Street,
Princeton, New Jersey 08540
In the United Kingdom: Princeton University Press, 6 Oxford Street,
Woodstock, Oxfordshire OX20 1TW
press.princeton.edu

Library of Congress Cataloging-in-Publication Data

Martí, José Luis, 1975–
A political philosophy in public life : civic republicanism
in Zapatero's Spain / José Luis Martí and Philip Pettit.
p. cm.
Includes bibliographical references and index.
ISBN 978-0-691-14406-1 (hardcover : alk. paper)
1. Republicanism—Spain. 2. Rodríguez Zapatero, José Luis, 1960–
3. Spain—Politics and government—1982–
I. Pettit, Philip, 1945– II. Title.
JN8210.M37 2010
320.01—dc22

British Library Cataloging-in-Publication Data is available

This book has been composed in Sabon

Printed on acid-free paper. ∞

Printed in the United States of America

1 3 5 7 9 10 8 6 4 2

CONTENTS

PREFACE

POLITICAL THEORY AND POLITICAL practice occupy different worlds, operating in spaces that are as discontinuous as the many universes postulated in science fiction or string theory. And yet wormholes occasionally open between those spaces, providing temporary portals and creating the possibility of some traffic across the divide. This book is an attempt to record one such opening and to reflect on its more general significance.

After his election to the leadership of the Spanish socialist party in 2000, José Luis Rodríguez Zapatero decided to explore academic philosophies in order to systematize his ideas for renewing his social democratic view of government. For a variety of reasons he settled on a formulation in terms provided by the tradition of civic republicanism, thereby connecting his philosophy of politics with a classical European heritage. Philip Pettit's book, *Republicanism: A Theory of Freedom and Government*, had just appeared in Spanish, and over the years that followed Zapatero and his allies in the party used it to develop the platform that they took into the 2004 election.

Mr. Zapatero won that election and soon afterward invited Pettit to give a lecture in Madrid on the civic republican view of government. This Pettit did in July 2004, outlining the central ideas in the republican approach and enumerating the challenges that Zapatero would have to face if he were to stick to the program. In his reply the prime minister insisted that he would be faithful to the program and, in token of his sincerity, publicly invited Pettit to assess the fidelity of his government to republican principles prior to the 2008 election. Pettit presented his review in a lecture that he gave in Madrid three years later, in June 2007.

The review appears as chapter 3 of this book, where it is filled out by responses to various queries that were raised among Spanish commentators and critics; these form an appendix to the chapter. The first of the two chapters that lead up to the review provides a full account of how the Spanish socialist party came to embrace civic republicanism and the second gives an outline of civic republican theory. The fourth chapter, immediately following the review, presents an extended interview with Prime Minister Zapatero on questions related to his program. And then the fifth and final chapter provides some general reflections on what is required for a political philosophy to be available for practical employment, indicating the strengths of civic republicanism in this regard. A Spanish book, *Examen a Zapatero*, which appeared shortly before the March 2008 election, included chapters 3 and 4 of this book together with a shorter, earlier version of chapter 2 (Pettit 2008).

The review of Zapatero's government is positive, finding that the intense program of legislation implemented in his first term in power fits extremely well with the desiderata that civic republicans highlight. There is no way of proving that the policies implemented were enacted for explicitly republican reasons, since we have no detailed information on how arguments transpired in party back rooms. But if Zapatero is to be taken at his word, and if the tenor of his public rhetoric is to be believed, then the fit between the policies he adopted and the principles of civic republicanism is hardly an accident.

Prime Minister Zapatero was returned to office in the election of March 2008 but we make no attempt in this book to explore how far he has remained faithful to the civic republican commitments he adopted in his first term. Since economic fortunes have now taken a severe downturn in Spain, as in the world at large, the best we may hope for in the short run is that he will at least consolidate the reforms that were put in place. He committed himself to doing this at the plenary congress of his party, the Partido Socialista Obrero Español (PSOE), in July 2008.

Nor does the book attempt to review legislation that occurred in the final months of Zapatero's first term in government. The main casualty here is the Law of Historical Memory, which was passed by the Spanish parliament and signed into law on October 31, 2007. This law reverses the agreement to bury the past that was an implicit part of the post-Franco settlement. It recognizes the victims of both sides in the Civil War and under Franco's regime but otherwise seeks to redress the balance of historical memory in favor of the opposition to Franco. Thus it denies legitimacy to Francoist laws and trials, prohibits political events at his burial place in the Valley of the Fallen, and provides state help for the exhumation of his victims (Treglown 2009).

It should be of some interest for readers to see what the Zapatero government achieved in its first term and that is one reason for wanting to publish this book. But we also hope that the book will be of interest for more general and perhaps more enduring reasons. We are committed to the civic republican research program in political philosophy, and we see this book as contributing to reflection on what that program requires in institutional terms. Those with similar commitments, or those with an interest in interrogating the claims of civic republicanism, may find the book worthwhile for similar reasons. We also hope that the book may offer some stimulus for thinking about the general connection between political theory and political practice—and about how far theory can or should seek to be nonutopian—since it offers a case study in how linkages may be forged.

The bulk of the book was prepared in the academic year 2008–9, when José Luis Martí was a Laurance S. Rockefeller Visiting Fellow at the University Center for Human Values at Princeton. This fellowship gave us the opportunity to work closely together and we are grateful to Princeton University for making it possible. We are also grateful to many friends and colleagues who have helped us through various stages of preparation. Those to whom we are separately indebted are mentioned in two notes at the beginning of chapters 1 and 3, respectively. Those to whom we are jointly indebted include David Casassas, Robert Fishman, Philipp

Koralus, Victoria McGeer, Jan Werner Muller, Amalia Amaya Navarro, Águeda Quiroga, and Fernando Vallespín. We have learned a great deal from some communications with William Chislett, author of a regular newsletter for the Real Instituto Elcano (Chislett 2004–9)—these newsletters figure prominently in our references—and of a recent book on Spain (Chislett 2008). We were productively challenged by exchanges with Pedro J. Ramírez, Felipe Sahagún, and other *El Mundo* colleagues. And we benefited from an exchange with Prime Minister Zapatero, and from separate exchanges with Minister Moratinos, as well as ex-Ministers Aguilar and Caldera, in the wake of the review. Perhaps our greatest debt is to José Andrés Torres Mora, a member of the Spanish Parliament and an adviser to Zapatero; he has been a constant source of information, advice, and encouragement. Special thanks are owed to Julie Scales, who patiently and efficiently proofread chapter 1 and helped to translate the interview with Zapatero, and to the readers of the manuscript for Princeton University Press who passed on a wealth of useful feedback. Finally, we must record our gratitude to Ian Malcolm of Princeton University Press whose support for the venture was essential both in its genesis and in its completion.

A POLITICAL PHILOSOPHY IN PUBLIC LIFE

1

THE SPANISH CONTEXT

JOSÉ LUIS MARTÍ[1]

JOSÉ LUIS RODRÍGUEZ ZAPATERO, prime minister of Spain,[2] has affirmed on several occasions that he endorses and is inspired by the political philosophy of civic republicanism, and specifically by the work of Philip Pettit. As Zapatero has stated: "this modern political philosophy called republicanism ... is very important nourishment to what we want for our country" (Prego 2001, 166). Consequently, both civic republicanism and Pettit's name have been present in the Spanish media and debates in recent years, being widely and critically discussed by both the Left and the Right. José Andrés Torres Mora, one of Zapatero's closest advisers, who is also a sociologist and deputy in the Spanish Congress, describes Pettit's influence in these terms: "Philip Pettit provided us with the appropriate grammar to furnish our political intuitions, to express the kind of proposals and dreams we had in mind for Spain. Pettit's republicanism has been our north star" (Torres Mora 2008).

This is the first time in recent history, to my knowledge, that any political leader has unambiguously embraced civic republicanism. Some obvious questions raised then are: Why did Zapatero commit himself to such a political philosophy just after his 2000 election as Secretary General of the Spanish Socialist Workers' Party (Partido Socialista Obrero Español or PSOE)? Why did Zapatero feel the need to engage a concrete political philosophy? And why has Pettit's theory been considered "important nourishment," "the appropriate grammar," and the "north star" for Zapatero's policies in Spain? These are some of the questions I am going to address in the present chapter, as I rehearse the main events in the history of Zapatero's Spain relative to his endorsement of such a political philosophy.[3] The chapter will set the scene for the rest of the book, particularly for chapters 3 and 4.

Zapatero's commitment might be surprising to many people—as surprising as it was in Spain in 2000. Yet it made sense in the context of the new millennium. After three decades of neoliberal dominance and the random mixing of neoliberal ideas with more traditional social democratic commitments, as in the case of Tony Blair's Third Way, social democracy was faced with an ideological crisis. In this impoverished context, civic republicanism (or civicism, as Pettit has also called it) has obvious attractions as a way of grounding social democracy. It is based on the value of freedom, offering a normative philosophy that challenges neoliberalism or libertarianism in its own preferred terms.[4] In endorsing civic republicanism, Zapatero opposed libertarianism and right-wing liberalism more generally, as well as the Third Way and other philosophical ways of rethinking social democracy. He opted for a modest but powerful new foundation for the Left.

In what follows I shall speak frequently of the civic republican ideal of freedom as nondomination. The notion is fully explained in chapter 2, but it may be useful to offer a brief characterization here. Freedom as nondomination is contrasted, in Pettit's work, with freedom as noninterference. Two points explain the contrast. First, you may enjoy freedom as nondomination and yet suffer some interference, such as the interference of coercive law. That sort of interference will not reduce your freedom to the extent that the law is under your control as a member of the citizenry and does not impose an alien will: it is nonarbitrary, to use a favorite republican phrase. But, as you may suffer interference without being dominated so, to go to the second point of contrast, you may be dominated—you may be subject to the will of others—without suffering any actual interference. This will happen to the extent that others can impose their will, should they take against your pattern of choice, but do not do so because of being content with your choices. What you choose in such a situation, you choose by their leave. It may be sheer luck that you do not attract their interference, and that you enjoy their leave to choose as you do, or it may be the product of a self-censoring strategy; you may shape your choices so as to keep them sweet.

Subjection to the arbitrary will of others is exemplified in Roman tradition by the position of the servant or *servus* in relation to the master or *dominus*; hence the talk of freedom as nondomination. The ideal of freedom as nondomination raises a dual challenge for the state. The state should provide protection against the private forms of domination that people may suffer as a result of disadvantage in any resources, legal, educational, financial, contractual, or cultural. Yet at the same time the state should be nondominating in how it relates to its people, giving them constitutionally and democratically mediated control over the policies and initiatives it adopts. It will have to interfere in their economic and other affairs in order to provide protection against domination, but the interference should be subject to popular control in a way that makes it nonarbitrary.

This ideal had strong appeal for Mr. Zapatero, as the interview in chapter 4 makes clear. It means that freedom is deeply connected with equality on the one hand, and with democracy on the other. As we shall see, Mr. Zapatero makes frequent reference to this ideal of freedom, presenting it not as something that thrives in the absence of government, but as an ideal that requires both the engagement of government in people's lives, and people's active contestation and vigilance. One particular aspect of the civic republican tradition that obviously caught Mr. Zapatero's attention was the eyeball test to which Pettit had drawn attention in his book (1997, 166; see also chapter 2 in this volume). According to this test you enjoy freedom in relation to others—to a particular other or to others as represented in a group or in a government—only insofar as you can look them in the eye, without fear or deference, with a shared consciousness of this equal status. You can command the respect of others and enjoy the dignity of an equal among equals.

Political Background

Spain has had two different socialist prime ministers in its recent democratic history: Felipe González and José Luis Rodríguez Zapatero,[5] both from the Partido Socialista Obrero Español.[6] Felipe González led the country for almost fourteen years, from 1982 to 1996, following a classic social democratic ideology, at least during his first three terms.[7] His popularity and charisma made it possible for him to win four consecutive elections.[8] Among his achievements, the most noteworthy are the consolidation of democracy, his contribution to the development of a nascent welfare state in Spain,[9] the modernization of the country, and Spain's entry to the European Economic Community (now the European Union) in 1986 and to NATO in 1988. His excellent connections with European leaders, especially with German Chancellor Helmut Kohl and the President of the French Republic François Mitterrand, aided in positioning Spain on the international forefront, making it more respected and better known around the world. But not all was well and good. A number of serious grievances contributed to an unpleasant and bitter end to González' political life. There was harsh opposition from Spanish labor unions, giving rise to several general strikes, some serious episodes of institutional corruption which came to light mainly during his last term, a public charge of collusion or even complicity with state terrorism directed mainly against the ETA (the Basque terrorist group),[10] and a highly controversial privatization of the major public industrial and energy companies.

In 1996, in his fifth election since he was elected in 1982 (his seventh election in total), González was defeated by José María Aznar, who had brought new life to the Partido Popular (PP), the main center-right party in Spain.[11] However, because González still maintained a certain degree of popularity, the PP was able to capture only 39% of the votes, just one point ahead of the PSOE, giving Aznar, once elected, a tiny majority in the Congress of Deputies. This obliged him to negotiate in order to reach agreements with other parliamentary groups, mainly the Basque and Catalan nationalist parties, to be elected as prime minister and to pass the government's legislative initiatives.[12] This situation probably explains why Aznar's first term was a period of slight reform and smooth transition. But Aznar led the PP to a second and much greater victory in 2000, winning 44% of the votes, ten points ahead of the PSOE, and obtaining an (absolute) majority of deputies. This strengthened his government and allowed him to rule freely and implement his agenda.

Helped by the creation of the main right-wing think tank in Spain, FAES, the PP in the Aznar era held two basic ideological allegiances: libertarianism and Catholic conservatism.[13] On the one hand, Aznar openly admired the way Ronald Reagan's and Margaret Thatcher's governments had applied neoliberal or libertarian ideas, deregulating markets and abstaining from intervention in a manner favored by the right-wing liberals in his party. On the other hand, Aznar maintained strong ties to conservative Spanish circles and identified with the American neoconservative movement connected with George W. Bush; indeed he became one of Bush's closest international friends and allies. As I will explain later, one of Aznar's most contested political decisions during his second term was to engage Spain in the second war in Iraq.[14] The most applauded achievements were the good macroeconomic indicators—a much lower unemployment rate, a zero budget deficit, very low inflation—the privatization of the last large state-owned companies, and the introduction of several tax cuts.

All this background is relevant because, as I will explain soon, one of Zapatero's first priorities was to differentiate himself from both González and Aznar. The PSOE was suffering a serious crisis in the post-González years, basically due to a lack of clear and unitary leadership.[15] There were several internal divisions in the party that finally crystallized after the PSOE's huge electoral defeat on March 12, 2000.[16] A few months later, at the thirty-fifth PSOE conference, the party had to elect a new secretary general, and there was a common perception that a complete renewal was required. Different groups in the party presented their own candidates: namely, José Bono, representing the traditional *aparato* still influenced by González; Matilde Fernández, representing the *reformista* sector; Rosa Díez, then a deputy in the European Parliament and a very well-known Basque politician; and José Luis Rodríguez Zapatero, supported by a recently constituted minority group "Nueva Vía" ("New Way"), formed by young members of the PSOE who had not taken part in any of González' governments.[17] Zapatero had been a deputy in congress since 1989— when he was only 26—and had been very active there, but he was practically unknown at that time to Spaniards, and even to his own party. Despite his outsider status in the race, however, he won the election.[18]

Once elected as secretary general on July 23, 2000, Zapatero gave his first address to the party conference, expressing some hopeful substantive commitments and previewing his personal style; both things would characterize his political performance later. For this reason, the speech deserves some attention here. The substantive commitments endorsed can be reduced to the values of freedom and democracy, and they were complemented by a personal style that emphasized the virtues of dialogue and a "good mood or disposition." But perhaps the most important idea underlying the whole address was the necessity of change: change for the party itself and change for Spanish society as a whole.[19] Zapatero, as the new socialist leader, needed to differentiate himself from González and from an administration that had left a legacy of corruption scandals, suspicions of connivance with state terrorism, high unemployment rates, and economic crisis.

In this context Zapatero flew solo: "beyond today, we have a lot of things to do, a lot of things to live. The best part of our lives is not in our *backpack*, in our *past*; the best day in our lives is still to come" (Rodríguez Zapatero 2000).[20] There was to be change, then, but not abrupt and disruptive change: "you have clearly demanded a change and I am decisively committing myself to make it possible. But don't forget, don't ever forget, that it must always be a *tempered change*" (Rodríguez Zapatero 2000).[21]

The two substantive fundamental values expressed in this speech were participatory, deliberative democracy and freedom, and in his view they were related to each other as well as to solidarity. This meant a departure from the usual ideological discourse in

González' PSOE, which had focused more centrally on equality. The new departure was present in Zapatero's view, even before he had explicitly endorsed civic republicanism:

> We are going to deepen democracy: more participation, more transparency, but also more responsibility because democracy is precisely the free reflection of the people's will.... We want, therefore, an active and cohesive democracy ... a democracy that has recovered the value of the citizenry and strengthens the commitment of all. This is what defines us [the socialists], this is what distinguishes us: our passion for solidarity and the realization of freedoms. (Rodríguez Zapatero 2000)[22]

The "value of the citizenry" and the ideals of "political participation" and "responsibility," according to Zapatero, were intertwined with the value of dialogue and deliberation, as they were with the ideal of freedom: "this *is* the socialist tradition, and even the socialist instinct: to fix problems through discussion of ideas, and then, at the end, enjoy freedoms" (Rodríguez Zapatero 2000). The emphasis on political dialogue was expressive of a more general but characteristic style, associated with attitudes of respect and tolerance.[23] The essence of this style can be found in the popular motto Zapatero constantly applied to himself for many years when confronting the Right: el *talante* (the *good mood* or *disposition*). In this vein, he proposed that his opposition to Aznar's government was to be "loyal, constructive and useful," a tempered and respectful style in stark contrast to the rude and, at times, somewhat harsh style of Aznar and of many members of Aznar's government; a new style ultimately characterized by what has been called his "endemic optimism" and a promise of hope.[24]

Only four years after the electoral defeat of Felipe González, in the midst of a deep crisis in his own party, and immediately after Aznar's huge electoral victory, Zapatero sought in these statements to differentiate himself from both González' legacy and Aznar's style. He proposed a tempered change, based on solid new substantive ideas of freedom and democracy in order to renovate and modernize Spanish social democracy, and a new *talante* for respectful dialogue and democratic deliberation. To finish this quick overview of the political background surrounding Zapatero's endorsement of civic republicanism, let me now turn briefly to the general ideological moment of the Left in Europe.

European social democracy, based on a Keynesian welfarist view and virtually hegemonic since the end of the Second World War, was perceived as being in crisis or at least as requiring a deep renewal, as was Spanish social democracy, which traditionally mirrored the European model. Among the factors contributing to the widespread perception of failure of this model, we find the great influence of Ronald Reagan's and Margaret Thatcher's neoliberalism during the 1980s, the collapse of the Soviet Union and the Iron Curtain at the end of that decade, along with the subsequent loss of an ideological point of reference,[25] and the economic crisis of welfare states in Europe at the beginning of the 1990s. This perception was so extensive that Margaret Thatcher coined a famous phrase, which became her mantra, the acronym for which was TINA: "There is no alternative."[26] She maintained that whatever the problems and imperfections of the free market and the state's abstention from intervention, there was no alternative to neoliberalism or libertarianism: no alternative, in effect, to widespread deregulation and the minimal state. This simple yet influential idea undermined the ideological basis of the welfare state and offered a powerful conservative philosophy that characterized most right-wing governments in Europe in the early 1990s and influenced many of their left-wing opponents; it was a philosophy associated with economists and thinkers such as Milton Friedman, Friedrich Hayek, and Robert Nozick.

But in the late 1990s a number of social democratic leaders took office in several European countries. To mention only the most important: in 1997 Tony Blair and Lionel Jospin were elected prime ministers of the United Kingdom and France, respectively; and in 1998 Gerhard Schroeder was elected chancellor of Germany.[27] All of them found a world dominated by neoliberalism and faced the necessity to rethink social democracy and reform the traditional welfare state as a response to the right-liberal challenges.[28] In those years, the aim of "modernizing the Left" became a strict requirement for any progressive leader in Europe. The best-known response to this requirement was Tony Blair's Third Way, a doctrine designed by the distinguished sociologist Anthony Giddens (1994, 1998).

As its very name points out, this doctrine was presented as a sort of midway point between right-liberalism and social democracy. According to Blair, the Third Way was not intended to split the difference between Right and Left, but claimed to be a "modernized social democracy ... founded on the values which have guided progressive politics for more than a century—democracy, liberty, justice, mutual obligation and internationalism."[29] One of this new doctrine's central aims was to generate widespread social agreement between the private and the public sectors, between the Right and the Left, between employers and employees. The object of such agreement was to create a "positive welfare system" granting some of the traditional protection to the disadvantaged, but avoiding free-rider abuses and encouraging autonomy and private initiative (Giddens 1998, 128). To make possible such an agreement with the Right, and in addition to the alleged values mentioned above, the Third Way was an unashamedly pragmatist doctrine; that is, it was an approach to public management whose agenda was "output driven," not "ideologically driven" (Temple 2000), not excessively committed to principles. It tried to respond to popular demands rather than to put a previous ideology-driven agenda into practice.[30] And it supported totally contextual arrangements that might be viewed as simply opportunistic and not easy to export to other countries or generalize to other situations. This commitment was certainly successful in its objective of being compatible with the Right, to the extent that it was even endorsed by the extreme right-wing Austrian leader Jörg Haider. But the question was whether it entailed any social democratic principle at all, or was "no more than election rhetoric, a marketing ploy with little substance," as some have argued (Vincent 1998, 48–58). Some even accused it of being an abdication to neoliberalism, "framed by and moving on terrain defined by Thatcherism" (Hall 1998). This feeling was captured by the historian Eric Hobsbawm in saying that Blair was no more than "Thatcher in trousers."[31]

The Endorsement of Civic Republicanism

Because the Third Way became the most prominent attempt to renew social democracy in the 1990s, it was natural for the supporters of Nueva Vía to look in that direction when they began to organize Zapatero's PSOE internal election campaign for secretary general in 2000. They were also proposing an ideological renovation of social democracy, and actually began to use some of the Third Way's ideas in shaping their program, particularly the claim for the center position in politics and the emphasis on the responsibility of the citizenry. Even the group's name resembled that of the British doctrine. Nevertheless, these figures soon realized that the Third Way was not the kind of philosophical grounding they required for Spain; and this for two reasons. The first reason for discontent was that the Third Way did not sufficiently differentiate them from González.[32] As the would-be deputy prime minister in Zapatero's government, María Teresa Fernández de la Vega, declared: "The Third Way in Spain was already done by González. And then we find the new way, the modernizing impulse, or whatever expression you prefer; 21st-century socialism: Zapatero's one" (de Toro 2007, 59).[33] As acknowledged by Zapatero, in the interview reproduced in chapter 4: "we were asked if we were going to follow Blair's way. We were the next generation of Spanish socialists, and were obliged to go beyond Felipe [González]" (see chapter 4). The second reason for discontent with the Third Way was that Zapatero and Nueva Vía were looking for a more refined and principled approach to social democracy—a solid ground for their political intuitions—and an approach that would connect with the writings and ideas of the first socialists in Spain, from whom they had drawn inspiration. The Third Way's pragmatism and ambiguity over neoliberalism made it unsatisfactory for these purposes.[34]

On October 19, 2000, shortly after his election as secretary general of the PSOE, José Luis Rodríguez Zapatero gave a lecture at the Club Siglo XXI, a prestigious intellectual forum in Madrid, with the aim of delineating the content of his "new socialism." There was a great deal of uncertainty and anticipation, in both the media and the civil society, a completely understandable reaction since, as pointed out above, Zapatero was a virtual unknown and he was facing the enormous challenge of renewing the PSOE. He and the Nueva Vía group were proposing an ideological transformation of social democracy in Spain. Thus, one of the most important aspects expected of Zapatero's speech was to clarify his ideological grounds, or to give at least a clue as to the direction that this transformation would take.

Along lines similar to those followed in his first address to the PSOE three months earlier, he advocated political aims such as the following: modernizing Spain; renewing social democracy; introducing a new style in politics based on respect and dialogue; ensuring authentic equality of opportunity to everyone; attending primarily to the most disadvantaged; and giving priority to public education as the most appropriate means to ensure the rectification of social inequalities and promote the autonomy of individuals. Zapatero also emphasized the idea that the twenty-first century "must be the beginning of an era of sovereign individuals, of a truly empowered citizenry, able to choose and build its own destiny," in a context of more democracy and more respect for freedom (quoted by Papell 2008, 32). These two values—freedom and democracy—were again at the center of his discourse; the goal of empowering the citizenry appeared for the first time. Zapatero seemed to be completely conscious of the sort of values he wanted to pursue if he won the election, and the whole speech was built around them.

But there was still a problem: he had yet to find an adequate and articulated philosophy for grounding such values. And perhaps for that reason he used a very ambiguous and polemic label for referring to his ideological stance, and by doing so caused considerable concern in Spain. His leadership in the PSOE, he asserted, was going to be "deeply and authentically liberal or, if you prefer, libertarian (*libertario*), and radically promoting individuals' equality" (quoted by Papell 2008, 32).[35] The adjective *libertario* in Spanish can mean two very different things, both of them quite alarming in a speech by the new social democratic leader in Spain, when referring to his proposed ideological renewal of Spanish social democracy. These two meanings are "anarchist" and far-right "liber-tarian."[36] Thus, the consequent polemic generated in the Spanish media increased the pressure on Zapatero to find a new philosophical basis for his ideas about the future of social democracy.

This was the context in which José Andrés Torres Mora, a sociologist and member of Nueva Vía, and someone very close to Zapatero, encouraged him to read Philip Pettit's book *Republicanism*. The republican tradition, he thought, could offer Spanish social democracy a solid philosophical basis. Zapatero read the book and was soon convinced that this doctrine was a good fit with his own principles and intuitions about freedom and democracy. In the words already quoted from Torres Mora (2008), "Philip Pettit provided us with the appropriate grammar to furnish our political intuitions, to express the kind of proposals and dreams we had in mind for Spain. Pettit's republicanism has been our north star." It is not that Zapatero and his colleagues were suddenly persuaded to be republican. They already cherished, at least broadly speaking, the values promoted by republicanism—freedom, equality, democracy, and the empowerment of the citizenry—as the rhetoric of Zapatero's first speeches shows. But their objectives were not sufficiently articulated. What they lacked was precisely the sort of philosophical elaboration and consistency that Pettit's book offered them. And contrary to some criticisms, as I will argue later in this chapter, civic republicanism was not a strange doctrine unconnected to Spain's own political or intellectual tradition. In Zapatero's own terms, Pettit's book "clearly and systematically presents an old tradition of thought that is not foreign to us. Moreover, it has a practical side to it that I find extraordinarily useful for political work" (chapter 4).[37]

A few weeks after the lecture at the Club Siglo XXI, Zapatero publicly endorsed civic republicanism and acknowledged the influence of Pettit's work on him. Some time afterward, in an interesting interview with *El Mundo*, one of the most important newspapers in Spain with a right-wing orientation, Zapatero dug deeper into this idea, trying to differentiate his civic republicanism from other competing social democratic doctrines, such as Blair's Third Way and Jospin's new socialism[38]:

The modern political philosophy called republicanism ... is very important nourishment to what we want for our country. I think that socialism must make an intellectual effort to think about the politics for the 21st century: the varieties of political organization, the structure of the political system, the channels for participation and for fostering something truly republican: the civic virtues manifested in political behavior and public debate, an attitude of great tolerance for individual autonomy, about new ways of living together, about now emergent values; and a strong defense of politics as a real instrument for changing people's lives, not to offer them an abstract new world, but to make everyone's world better and better, and to allow them to participate in defining it. (Prego 2001)

The interviewer highlighted Zapatero's defense of freedom as a central value and then asked him how in his view freedom could be reconciled with the Left, since promoting it seemed to produce social inequalities. This was Zapatero's reply:

The pursuit of freedom, of the human beings' capacity of choice in their own lives, is the ultimate end of the best progressive ideology. But to make this possible the value of equality must play its own role. For people to be politically free, they must be equal under the law. I see equality as an instrument for people's freedom.

Equality is always presumed to be a value of the Left; it is our essence ... [but] I am trying to recover the recognition of socialism's best origins: a progressive thought that values freedom as well as equality, and one that does not propose uniformity, but recognition of diversity. This is what it means to be republican. (Prego 2001)

What Zapatero was trying to emphasize is that freedom is neither alien to the socialist tradition, nor needs to be at odds with equality. This idea was actually captured by a simple and traditional dictum in Spanish socialism that he emphatically employed: "socialism is freedom" (de Toro 2007, 210). According to Zapatero, freedom is closely connected not only with equality, but also with democracy and with the empowerment of the citizenry. To have "good democratic patterns," for him, is to have "good patterns of freedom in any place of the community," to give freedom to women, to those "who do not share the sexual orientation of the majority," and so on. This is why he takes freedom to be "the most creative idea" in politics (de Toro 2007, 211), as the best way for "citizens to combat public and private despotism" (Campillo 2004, 301).[39]

Armed with this particular philosophy, Zapatero acted as the leader of the PSOE, in opposition to Aznar's government, for that entire term (2000–4) of the Congress of Deputies. These years were devoted to the tasks of reconstructing the party, consolidating the new philosophy adopted by the PSOE, raising a new style in the opposition, open to dialogue and agreement, and preparing for the election in 2004.[40] His performance in the debates on the state of nation[41] confirmed his commitment to this particular interpretation of freedom and democracy, and gave him the opportunity to gain confidence and assertiveness. Spaniards, according to polls, considered Zapatero the winner in some of these debates, even though Aznar's popularity was still very high. As I said earlier, Aznar's government was achieving excellent macroeconomic indicators at that time. Probably the most difficult issue for the PP government was the massive popular rejection of Spain's participation in the Iraq War. A number of demonstrations were held in several Spanish cities, protesting against what was considered a war contrary to international law. The most massive ones were on February 15, 2003, with three million participants in Madrid and Barcelona alone.[42] These demonstrations contributed to a wide rejection of Aznar's administration in some sectors of the citizenry, though he remained very popular in others. As the election approached, his successor as the PP candidate for Prime Minister, Mariano Rajoy, was still ahead in the polls.[43]

On March 11, 2004, three days before the election, Madrid suffered an Al-Qaeda terrorist attack where 191 people were killed and 1,858 injured. It was the worst terrorist attack in the entire history of Spain. Al Qaeda claimed it to be a response to the Spanish participation in the invasion of Iraq. The management of the crisis by the government was, according to many analysts, obscure and manipulative. The government's spokesman, Miguel Ángel Acebes, continually reiterated the hypothesis that it was an ETA attack, concealing the first evidence which had clearly pointed to Al Qaeda.[44] Very soon the international press (CNN, *The Times*, Radio France International, the *New York Times*) began to announce that Al Qaeda was responsible for the attack, provoking outrage and spontaneous protests by many sectors in Spain against the government's management and representation of the crisis.[45] It is widely accepted by analysts that this terrorist attack and the response of the government shifted the outcome of the election: the polls beforehand had showed a slight majority in favor of the Partido Popular, but the PSOE finally won the election with 43% of the votes, obtaining 164 seats in Congress, while the PP won 38% of votes and 148 seats.[46] With these results, the PSOE became the largest party in the Congress of Deputies, and was able to present José Luis Rodríguez Zapatero as a candidate for prime minister through the congressional investiture or nomination process.

NOMINATION PROCESS AND FIRST CONTACTS WITH PETTIT

On April 16, 2004, Zapatero was elected prime minister by the Spanish Congress of Deputies with 183 votes (out of 350), having the support of his own party as well as five smaller parties represented in the chamber.[47] His *discurso de investidura*—the speech opening the investiture or nomination process in the congress— contained an abundance of philosophical references, achieving a level of abstraction that is not usual in the Spanish chamber.[48] This nomination speech is usually of political interest since it possesses an important symbolic dimension: it contains the candidate's public declaration of his political goals for governing the country for the next four years. But for the first time in the Spanish chamber, a candidate for prime minister was articulating a program based on the values of freedom as nondomination and deliberative democracy, in a solemn representation of his commitment to civic republicanism.

In the first part of the speech (April 8), Zapatero introduced his idea of a "decent country," one "which redistributes the wealth it generates in a balanced way; decent because its citizens act with solidarity with those who need it most."[49] Furthermore, he highlighted the two most important features of "our democracy": "individual freedom and social solidarity" (Rodríguez Zapatero 2004b, 7). In the following sessions of the speech (April 9 and 15), five crucial axes of his program were developed: "the renovation of the public life; a European and Europeanist foreign policy; economic development based on education, research, and innovation, thus creating stable jobs; new social policies oriented to the new necessities of persons and families; and the development and extension of civil and political rights, and of the value of equality to live together in an advanced way" (Rodríguez Zapatero 2004c, 18).

The first of these axes was presented as an absolute hallmark of his future government. It stressed the significance of having a new political style based on democratic dialogue, of "revitalizing Parliament," of practicing "political pedagogy," of regulating public mass media, of ensuring transparency and citizen access to institutional information, and so on.[50] The other axes were related to republican values as well; namely, the need to improve and strengthen education (including civic education for citizens), the development and extension of individual rights, and the goal of ensuring equality (between men and women, between heterosexuals and homosexuals) (Rodríguez Zapatero 2004c, 16–23). The idea of freedom as nondomination played a central role in the speech. And Zapatero was fully aware that this kind of freedom is only possible in a civic democracy with active and critical citizens, characterized by pluralism and respect; one in which such citizens are able to be involved in "constant democratic deliberation" and to participate in politics every day.[51] The speech concluded with these eloquent words:

> Your Honors, I promised a tempered change for a time of citizens. To this end, if I obtain your trust, I will rule with resoluteness in the principles, through dialogue and for hope.... The laws I am going to promote will pursue the aim of no one living under *arbitrary domination*. In Cervantes' words, a government of "mar-

row and substance," a government that accompanies its citizens in their problems and dreams because some utopias deserve to be dreamt. Perhaps we will not attain them completely, but they will be the signposts on the path we have to walk. (Rodríguez Zapatero 2004c, 24)[52]

Zapatero took office in the Moncloa, the residence and office of the Spanish prime minister, on April 17, 2004. His first, well-known decision, as widely promised during the campaign, was to withdraw the peacekeeping troops from Iraq, abandoning a war that he had denounced as unjust and in breach of international laws; he did this, it must be remembered, at the cost of jeopardizing the relationship with the United States, or at least with the people leading its government.[53] Not so well known was another move: he invited Philip Pettit, his mentor (as he was called by the Spanish media), to come to Spain. In July 2004, Pettit participated in several workshops in Madrid and afterward in Barcelona.[54] He lectured on the republican principles of government, explaining the content and implications of the central principle of freedom as nondomination, as well as its general requirements in terms of constitutionalism, self-government, rule of law, and civic virtue and engagement.

In one of these lectures, organized and funded by the Vodafone Foundation in the beautiful Círculo de Bellas Artes, a solemn cultural institution in Madrid, Pettit was hosted by Zapatero himself (this was their first personal meeting).[55] In this and other appearances, Pettit introduced the term "civism" in order to avoid a general misunderstanding in Spain concerning the word "republicanism."[56] This term was subsequently translated into Spanish differently depending on the medium or the speaker: the alternatives used were *civismo*, *ciudadanismo*, or *civicismo*.[57] Pettit also suggested an important and powerful metaphor for explaining to the people the point of republicanism or civism: the eyeball test. The goal of this political philosophy is to ensure that "everyone can look the others in the eye," without fear or deference, and with a shared consciousness of equal status. This is, in the end, what to be undominated means. A free citizen, in that sense, is able to require respect from others and to feel equal to them, to enjoy the same dignity and status, independent of economic, cultural, or personal differences (Pettit 1997, 166).

Pettit reminded Zapatero that the government's first obligation is to keep some individuals from being subjected to the will of other individuals, that is, to protect against private domination. But a second obligation, he argued, is no less important: to avoid public domination in the exercise of public power by government. Not only must government pursue progressive goals in the campaign against domination; it must also foster and recognize public controls and checks on its own performance.

Pettit expressed some skepticism about the possibility for a prime minister to remain true to republican principles, when all the pressures and incentives of politics were liable to push in another direction.[58] But Zapatero reiterated in public, in reply to that lecture, that he would not shrink from following where the approach led. And, as proof of this, he invited Pettit to review his government's performance at the end of the political term, to determine how far he had been faithful to the republican tradition.[59]

This was the origin of the relationship between the philosopher and the Prime minister.[60] The first version of Pettit's review came in the form of a lecture in June 2007, held first at the Centro de Estudios Constitucionales in Madrid, and then at the Instituto de Estudios Sociales Avanzados in Córdoba.[61] Afterward, the text of this lecture, supplemented with other material, including an interview with Zapatero, was published in book form in Spanish under the title *Examen a Zapatero*.[62]

A PRINCIPLED POLITICS FOR ZAPATERO'S FIRST POLITICAL TERM

Zapatero has claimed to be a principled political leader committed to the philosophy of civic republicanism and to a republican agenda. To judge whether that claim is sound is not my task here, since it is covered by Pettit in chapter 3.[63] But I want to offer three different examples of how Zapatero justified his major political decisions on the basis of his claim for a principled politics, one particularly oriented to the goal of reducing domination. I take these examples to show not that Zapatero is *really* a principled political leader, nor that he *sincerely* believes in civic republicanism (something that as a matter of fact I have no reasons to doubt), but at least that he *frequently uses* republican arguments to justify his major policies.[64] But before turning to these three examples, let me say a few words about the general political context at that time.

Zapatero's first term was not a peaceful or easy period of Spanish politics. It began with the immediate consequences of the worst terrorist attack ever suffered in Spain, on March 11, 2004. He also had to deal, among other things, with a ceasefire (March 23, 2005) and the following negotiation with ETA,[65] which was broken by a huge bombing in Madrid's airport, killing two people and destroying part of a new terminal (December 30, 2006). However, the main source of political tension and polarization was undoubtedly the Partido Popular's harsh and aggressive style of opposition. This is what has been called in Spain the politics of *crispación* (or harshening).[66] Perhaps inspired, as many analysts have stated, by the belligerent and openly hostile but successful opposition made by Aznar to González in his last term (1993–96), Mariano Rajoy, then leader of the PP, adopted a policy of making harsh accusations against the government, and of refusing to reach agreement with it on any issue. The PP was particularly aggressive on two fronts: the government's management of the ETA ceasefire and its sponsorship of territorial decentralization in Spain.[67]

Once ETA had announced a ceasefire and declared its willingness to reach some agreement for peace, Zapatero asked Congress to authorize the opening of negotiations with them, and was quite optimistic about the possibility of reaching a negotiated solution.[68] But the PP categorically rejected any sort of negotiation with terrorists—which was actually surprising, since Aznar himself had held his own conversations with the group when he was in office.[69] As this rejection hardened, the PP became ever more hostile, or even aggressive, in criticizing the government's decisions and policies. According to them, the government was offending the victims of the ETA's terrorist attacks with its attempt to achieve a negotiated solution to this problem. Some PP leaders frequently accused the government of "helping the terrorists" and even suggested that they were guilty of active connivance. Unlike the other political parties who all supported the negotiations, the PP was solely responsible for creating a general climate of tension and division that was hardly conducive to the success of the enterprise. Despite Zapatero's optimism, the ETA broke the ceasefire, as mentioned, in December 2006.

On the territorial as distinct from the terrorist issue, the PP protested that Zapatero was promoting a general program of reform in existing *Estatutos de Autonomía* (Statutes of Autonomy), the goal being to return more power to the Autonomous Communities.[70] But this project of significantly increasing the political autonomy of the communities was, according to the PP and other impartial analysts, dubiously constitutional. The new Statutes of Autonomy were certainly pushing territorial decentralization in Spain to its constitutional limits—and perhaps beyond them.[71] Even though the reforms were not initiated by the government itself, they were designed and supported by the PSOE or its affiliated parties, with the Catalan Socialist Party playing a special role in the process in Catalonia. Zapatero and the government, in any case, clearly admitted that they were pursuing a federalist agenda for Spain. All this provoked a long, general, and very aggressive PP campaign to try to stop the process.[72] Its central claim was that Zapatero's complicity with nationalists was breaking the country apart: "balkanizing" it, in a favorite phrase, and threatening an end thereby to the unity, by some accounts the existence, of the Spanish state.

In this atmosphere of parliamentary aggression and tension, Zapatero argued for a principled politics based on civic republicanism. His republicanism supported the dialogue that he pursued with ETA and the decentralization of power that increased regional autonomy would provide. But I choose three other examples to illustrate the republican direction of his thinking; it was not Zapatero's government, after all, that initiated dialogue with ETA or regional decentralization and neither was an essential part

of his electoral program.[73] I pick two examples related to his social agenda, and a third in the area of foreign policy. Each policy
to be illustrated was a part of Zapatero's political program, each
was developed in his first period of government, and each carried
a serious electoral risk. Together, then, they provide good evidence
of a principled politics.[74]

The first case I want to highlight is the June 2005 reform of the
civil code to include and regulate same-sex marriage in exactly the
same way as different-sex marriage. This was, of course, a very
controversial initiative, both socially and politically. The surprising fact is that when Zapatero announced his desire to carry out
this reform in his election campaign, the issue had not previously
been on the agenda. Nobody was expecting him to pursue permitting same-sex marriage, at least not in his first term.[75] Introducing
this initiative later, under more favorable conditions, would have
had no political cost for him. It is remarkable, then, that instead
of avoiding a potentially troublesome topic, Zapatero actively
pursued it, even in the face of very strong and united criticism.
The Spanish Catholic Church,[76] the whole Right, and even part of
his own party on the Left were fiercely opposed to it.[77] Furthermore, almost everybody, including some of those on the Left who
in principle favored the measure, questioned the urgency of such
a divisive initiative. But Zapatero went ahead with it, presenting
the initiative as a means of enlarging rights, protecting freedom
equally for all, and defending human dignity. In his defense of the
initiative in congress on June 30, 2005 he declared:

> After us will come many other countries, your honors, moved by
> two unstoppable forces: freedom and equality ... we are building a
> more *decent country* because a decent society is one that does not
> humiliate its members.... . Today Spanish society is responding to
> people who have been humiliated, to people whose rights have been
> ignored, their identity denied, and their freedom repressed. Today
> Spanish society gives them back the respect they deserve, recogniz-
> ing their rights, restoring their dignity, affirming their identity and
> restoring their freedom. It is true that they are only a minority, but

their victory is the victory for all. It is a victory even for those who oppose this reform, even when they are not aware of it. Their victory makes all of us better; it makes our society better. (Rodríguez Zapatero 2005, 5228, emphasis added)

The second example I want to mention is one of Zapatero's major initiatives regarding the welfare state: the design and approval of the Dependency Act in November 2006. This was intended to provide economic and personal assistance to those people with high degrees of dependency on others, for instance the dependency that can derive from physical or mental impairment. The Spanish welfare state traditionally left the kind of care and assistance that these people needed in the hands of their families or friends, placing an unfair burden on them and at the same time giving rise to dependency and facilitating domination. The Dependency Act was intended to produce a new pillar of the welfare state, aimed at those people with physical or mental handicaps.[78] It would grant new rights to citizens, not as an act of mercy or benevolence, but with the explicit goal of reducing the domination of a significant part of the Spanish citizenry.[79] The Dependency Act involved a major reform of the Spanish welfare state, one that was expensive and continues to be controversial.[80] Although there was no very significant pressure for developing it,[81] Zapatero embraced the reform as an essential part of a republican program.[82]

My third example concerns Zapatero's foreign policy and more concretely his foundation of the Alliance of Civilizations. From the very beginning of his first term as prime minister, Zapatero had to differentiate his foreign policy from Aznar's. As mentioned, his first decision as prime minister was to withdraw the Spanish troops sent to Iraq by Aznar in support of the American invasion, a war considered by him as illegal under international legal standards and as lacking the authorization of the United Nations.[83] However, despite vast popular support, his decision was strongly opposed by the Right in Spain, and it caused an openly tense personal relationship with George Bush and Tony Blair, which in turn affected Spain's foreign policy with some of its immediate allies. In this scenario, the most important international initiative made by Zapatero's government, leaving aside his participation in several European Union processes and initiatives, was the creation of an international Alliance of Civilizations (AoC) under the auspices of the United Nations. This multilateral project works to bring different cultures and sensibilities together, with an explicit emphasis on bridging the gaps between Western and Islamic countries.[84]

The idea was personally launched by Zapatero in the United Nations' fifty-ninth General Assembly on September 21, 2004. The AoC's three main objectives are (1) to "develop a network of partnerships with States, international organizations, civil society groups, and private sector entities that share the goals of the Alliance of Civilizations, to reinforce their interaction and coordination with the United Nations' system," (2) to develop, support and highlight projects that promote understanding among cultures," primarily regarding "youth, education, media and migration," and (3) to establish relations and facilitate dialogue among groups that can act as a force of moderation during times of heightened cross-cultural tensions."[85] With these goals, the alliance aims to be the seed of an international framework of dialogue for promoting the values of democracy, tolerance, and freedom in the international sphere. Zapatero's proposal sought to create an international space in which there might be a viable concept of an international public interest—a global common good. The idea was to combat the tendency for international action and policy to reflect only particular, sectional interests.

These three examples illustrate the role that civic republicanism played in Zapatero's public justification of his policies and initiatives. This still leaves open the question of whether these initiatives can be considered as truly republican—a question that will be faced in chapter 3. Before concluding this chapter, however, let me deal with two issues that have been postponed in previous sections: first, the connection between civic republicanism and the Spanish political tradition; and second, the impact of Zapatero's endorsement of republicanism on Spanish public debate.

CIVIC REPUBLICANISM IN THE SPANISH POLITICAL TRADITION

In his conversations with the Spanish writer Suso de Toro, José Luis Rodríguez Zapatero declared: "Spain, for me, is democracy. The axis of my vision of Spain is a democratic conception of the political community. The Spain which succeeded in the past and will succeed in the future is the Spain of living together with tolerance and respect" (de Toro 2007, 160). He added: "The socialist tradition that I prefer is the tradition of democratic thinking, of civic republicanism, of all that is related to the Institución Libre de Enseñanza.... If I have to define myself using only a couple of political terms, I would say I am a 'social democrat'; and absolutely proud of being a socialist" (de Toro 2007, 210). As mentioned above, Zapatero and his advisors in Nueva Vía found in Pettit's civic republicanism the appropriate grammar for reinterpreting socialism and expressing their own political intuitions and principles concerning freedom and democracy. And, importantly, they did not see such doctrine as unconnected with, or alien to, their own Spanish political tradition. Rather, it was the heir to important historical precedents in the Spanish socialist political tradition, as well as connected to what many contemporary scholars were advocating in Spain.

Zapatero finds the historical origins of his particular, republican way of relating freedom as nondomination, equality, and democracy with one another in the social and cultural movement of the 1920s and 1930s in Spain[86] that was organized around the Institución Libre de Enseñanza. This was rooted in the formation of Spanish socialist thinking in the late nineteenth and early twentieth centuries by authors like Pablo Iglesias, Francisco Giner de los Ríos, Indalecio Prieto, and Julián Besteiro.[87] According to Zapatero, "the republicans, the socialism of that time, the democratic thinking, includes the theory which assumes that all common order for living together aspires to make sure that no one feels dominated."[88] These first socialist thinkers emphasized the compatibility between socialism and the value of freedom, or what they took at that time to be liberalism.[89]

The connection between socialism and a republican understanding of freedom should not be surprising. One of the reasons why the republican tradition was not present as such in the second half of the nineteenth century and a good part of the twentieth is that socialism was leading in the defense of freedom as nondomination and democracy. This can be tracked in the works of major social democratic thinkers like Eduard Bernstein (1850–1932), one of the editors of the influential German magazine *Sozialdemokrat* and one of the authors of the Erfurt Program in 1891. His idea of an evolutionary socialism (1899), for instance, contained much of a defense of freedom and democracy as the proper socialist values which contribute to emancipation (Bernstein 1909, part III). The works of Eduard Bernstein, not well known today in the United States or Spain, were very important during that time and arrived in Spain through the influence of Krausism, a determinant doctrine for the formation of Spanish socialist thinking.[90] Relevant figures such as Gumersindo de Azcárate, Joaquín Costa, Manuel Sales i Ferré, and above all Adolfo Posada (1860–1944) defended freedom while opposing liberalism and gave it a social perspective connected to democracy which was central for building Spanish socialism.[91]

One of the effects of Krausism's influence in Spain was the creation, by Azcárate and Giner de los Ríos among others, of the Institución Libre de Enseñanza, in Madrid in 1876. This was an educational institution characterized by a great freedom in choosing the contents of the courses received by students and by being open to outside influence. It was the most important center for renovating ideas in Spain, having a great impact on the whole society prior to the Civil War in 1936. Among the first graduates, for instance, are many of the relevant figures of the Spanish thinking of that time, like Leopoldo Alas Clarín, Julián Besteiro, Joaquín Costa, Manuel Batolomé Cossío, Fernando de los Ríos, José Ortega y Gasset, Gregorio Marañón, and Adolfo Posada. Also worth mentioning is the distinguished list of poets, writers, and artists who studied there: Juan Ramón Jiménez, Federico García Lorca, Antonio Machado, Luis Buñuel, and Salvador Dalí were among the most prominent. This center articulated a rich vein of democratic thinking in the

Spanish Left which finally came to life in the short-lived Second Republic, providing a crucial counterbalance to the more radical trends existing in Marxism and anarchism.[92]

Considering these important precedents in the Spanish left-wing tradition, it is not surprising that civic republicanism had a long history among Spanish scholars as well as important figures nowadays. Two different generations of sociologists, political theorists, and philosophers have proved to be deeply interested by civic republicanism, and have analyzed and defended its principles and values, producing a rich and ever-increasing body of literature on the topic. The list of contributors is long, and includes names such as Salvador Giner, Félix Ovejero, Fernando Vallespín, Andrés de Francisco, Victoria Camps, Adela Cortina, Antoni Doménech, Aurelio Arteta, Ramón Vargas-Machuca, José Rubio-Carracedo, David Cassassas, Francisco Herreros, Teresa Montagut, Helena Béjar, Dani Raventós, and Ramón Ruiz Ruiz. They all work in different disciplines and at different universities, frequently without much contact with each other, but they nonetheless form one of the most important groups of political thinkers in Spain, with frequent presence in Spanish journals, newspapers, and books. Many of these authors applauded Zapatero's commitment to republicanism and aided in explaining to the people the ideals contained in the republican tradition, thus enriching the public debate.

THE IMPACT OF ZAPATERO'S ENDORSEMENT ON SPANISH PUBLIC DEBATE

Zapatero's explicit endorsement of civic republicanism, as articulated by Philip Pettit, ensured that both the philosophy and the philosopher received considerable attention from both foes and allies in newspapers, radio, television, and other digital media. While the arguments made in the Spanish public sphere were not always deep or principled, there were some remarkable discussions inaugurated by journalists and scholars. I will not offer here a proper and comprehensive analysis of the impact that Zapatero's endorsement of civic republicanism had in the Spanish public debate, but I will give some examples of the kind of arguments and discussions developed in mass media, especially in the most important newspapers, as proof of the interest generated in Spain around civic republicanism and Pettit's ideas.

As pointed out in the last section, Spain has a long and rich tradition of scholars advocating different versions of republicanism. Many of these scholars were already contributing to the public debate in newspapers and other media before Zapatero endorsed Pettit's brand of republicanism. These writers intensified their contributions once the word "republicanism" began to appear everywhere in the political sections of principal newspapers. Not all of them were satisfied with Zapatero's declared allegiances, of course: first, because they were still not totally sure about his sincerity; and second because not all were equally satisfied with the particular version of republicanism defended by Pettit. But, regardless of whether the ultimate end was to celebrate or to complain about Zapatero's endorsement, many left-wing intellectuals actually made an effort to explain to the Spanish public what civic republicanism meant.[93]

Much of what appeared from the Right in this public debate amounted, as might be expected, to politics by other means. In a reflection of the tension in Spanish politics and the *crispación* practiced by the PP, Zapatero's political philosophy and even Pettit himself were exposed to tough and sometimes offensive criticism. If Zapatero was invoking a political philosophy on which to base his decisions and initiatives, the unsurprising priority of the opposition was to discredit or reject this approach. But notwithstanding these pressures, some journalists and right-wing intellectuals developed honest and thorough discussions of civic republicanism, opening debates with advocates of the approach, and generating an unusually sophisticated debate in the Spanish public sphere.

One of the earliest reactions to Zapatero's endorsement of civic republicanism was that of Álvaro Delgado-Gal in an article in *El País*, the leading daily newspaper in Spain and generally favorable to socialists. In this commentary republicanism was likened to a rabbit being pulled out of Zapatero's socialist hat (Delgado-Gal 2001).[94] The main point was to suggest a sort of dilemma for

Zapatero. Either he was being hypocritical in endorsing a doctrine that was designed just to win more votes, or he was ignorant of the commitment taken on; according to the author republicanism was plainly "a bad model" and an ineffective basis for criticizing liberalism.[95] This early article drew responses from some Spanish advocates of republicanism, discussing remarkably abstract issues like the appropriateness of Berlin's distinction between positive and negative liberty, or whether there was room for a third conception of liberty, freedom as nondomination.[96] It is worth mentioning Delgado-Gal's article because it foreshadowed a series of attacks from the Right, the target of which was sometimes Rodríguez Zapatero, sometimes civic republicanism, and sometimes Pettit himself.[97]

Regarding Zapatero, the usual argument was to portray the prime minister as strategically hypocritical, as someone who by endorsing civic republicanism was only carrying out a marketing campaign, invoking an ancient, acclaimed philosophy for his own political benefit. This objection was no doubt prompted by the fact that it was very rare for a political leader in Spain—rare indeed for a political leader anywhere—to endorse a well-defined political philosophy. It must have been natural for many to think that this could not be a sincere move, only a self-serving public-relations strategy.[98]

The second target in this debate was the political philosophy of civic republicanism itself. Even if Zapatero was sincere in his endorsement of this theory, according to this second line of attack, the theory itself was inappropriate. Once again a dilemma dominated the debate. Either the republican proposals were reasonable, emphasizing the rule of law and the protection of rights, and casting freedom as nondomination as just a variety of negative freedom, in which case they added nothing to liberalism, or civic republicanism differed substantially from liberalism, in which case it could not count as reasonable.[99]

The third target of attack was Pettit himself. Even if Zapatero was being honest and civic republicanism was somehow appropriate, the version defended by Pettit was definitely not the right one.

Or, even worse, he was not a philosophically detached defender; by some accounts he was just a party hack.[100]

In the midst of this offensive from the Right, there was an important journalist who paid considerable attention to this philosopher and his theory. Pedro J. Ramírez, editor in chief of the liberal right-wing newspaper *El Mundo*, devoted three extensive articles in his influential Sunday column to Pettit and his connection with Zapatero, as well as writing many other pieces in which Pettit figured marginally. Two of these long articles contained faithful explanations of some republican principles defended by Pettit, such as the rule of law, the conditions of a mixed constitution, and the very protection of freedom as nondomination, arguing that Zapatero's actions did not conform properly to them (Ramírez 2006a,b). The third article was of quite a different tenor. It was an open letter to Pettit addressing the content of his civic audit of the government, three weeks before the first public lecture. Ramírez had somehow obtained a copy of the text and attacked its claims, prior to the lecture itself (Ramírez 2007). The article argued that Pettit had not been informed or had been misinformed about what was truly going on in Spain. Ramírez offered his own description of the facts to be assessed, and finally challenged Pettit to take that description into account in his lectures and publications.[101] Although there was a possible political motivation for these arguments, there was some value in the questions and objections raised. Pettit decided to respond to them in the book *Examen a Zapatero*; and the response is also included as an appendix to chapter 3 in the present book.

The endorsement by Prime Minister Rodríguez Zapatero of the political philosophy of civic republicanism—his adoption of civic republicanism as "an appropriate grammar" for developing his political initiatives—had a considerable impact on Spanish public debate. Perhaps, as the critics suggested, it had something to do with marketing, or with delivering a name, even a label, to rectify the mistake made in the lecture at the Club Siglo XXI. But whatever the real motivations Zapatero happened to have, what is important here is what he actually did, the decisions he made and the initiatives he pursued.. If a government claims to be republican, the question is whether it operates in conformity to republican principles. And if it does operate in that way, then for all practical purposes—for all purposes that matter from our viewpoint in this book—it is republican. This opens the way for the review of Zapatero's performance in chapter 3. Before coming to that review, however, it will be useful to provide an overview of civic republican philosophy, and this is the topic of chapter 2.

2

CIVIC REPUBLICAN THEORY

PHILIP PETTIT

THIS CHAPTER SEEKS TO provide an overall, accessible view of the traditional, republican philosophy of freedom and government, presenting it as an alternative to better-established liberal views, whether of a left-of-center or right-of-center cast. I describe the philosophy as civic republican, relying on the "civic" tag to mark three contrasts; they might also be marked by use of the word "civicism," a neologism that has a certain currency. The first is a contrast with mere opposition to monarchy, something that is important in a constitutional monarchy like Spain or the United Kingdom. The second is a contrast with the republicanism of the American political party. And the third is a contrast with communitarian forms of so-called republican thought in which the central ideals are popular sovereignty and universal participation in its exercise. In these versions of republican thought, born of eighteenth- and nineteenth-century romanticism, individual freedom is identified with participation in the formation of the collective, sovereign will of the community.

Civic republicanism in my preferred sense is defined by the rather more sober historical tradition that goes back to republican Rome. The historical work of Zera Fink (1962), Caroline Robbins (1959), and John Pocock (1975) revived interest in classical republican writers and established the continuity of the republican tradition through Renaissance Europe, seventeenth-century England, and revolutionary America. Building on that body of research, Quentin Skinner showed that in this tradition the master idea of freedom was not cast in the communitarian manner, as had been generally taken for granted, but in a more negative way. It was conceptualized, not as the positive benefit of participation in sovereign self-rule, but as a negative good that such participation might instrumentally serve: the good of escaping the imposition of others (Skinner 1984, 1985, 1990a,b).

The tradition that these historians identified and charted might be described as Mediterranean-Atlantic republicanism, since the figures who occupy the most prominent places are classical Roman authors, medieval Italian thinkers, and seventeenth- and eighteenth-century English-speaking writers from Britain and America. That tradition might be contrasted with the Franco-Prussian form that republicanism assumed in the work of Rousseau and Kant, and in later thinkers who wrote under their influence or in reaction to them. The later adherents of this variant form of republicanism embraced the notion of freedom as participation in sovereign self-rule but in the earlier tradition—in republicanism, period, as we may say—liberty is associated with the absence of interpersonal imposition.

But what sort of imposition was taken in this Mediterranean-Atlantic tradition to be inimical to freedom? The answer that has come to be widely accepted among contemporary historians and defenders of the tradition is the domination whereby one person has a certain mastery in the life of another (Pettit 1996, 1997; Skinner 1998). The idea of freedom as nondomination is now the crucial unifying theme for those who work within the civic republican framework, though of course within that frame there are also some differences of emphasis and detail (Pettit 2002).

This chapter begins with an attempt to explain what domination means and what freedom as nondomination therefore implies. The concept of freedom as nondomination marks a contrast with liberal approaches that, as we shall see, generally take freedom to require noninterference. Because it is primarily focused on the fate of individual citizens, it also marks a contrast with any more communitarian philosophy.

THE DOMINATION COMPLAINT

Think of how you feel when your welfare depends on the decision of another and you have no comeback against that decision. You are in a position where you will sink or swim, depending on the other's say-so; and you have no physical or legal recourse, no recourse even in a network of mutual friends, against that other. You are in the other's hands; you are at the other's mercy.

This experience of subjection to another comes in many forms (Lovett, forthcoming). Think of the child of the emotionally volatile parent; the wife of the occasionally violent husband; or the pupil of the teacher who forms arbitrary likes and dislikes. Think of the employee whose security requires keeping the boss or manager sweet; the debtor whose fortunes depend on the caprice of moneylender or bank manager; or the owner of a small business whose viability depends on the attitude taken by a bigger competitor or a union boss. Think of the welfare recipient whose fortunes turn on the mood of the counter clerk; the immigrant or indigenous person whose standing is vulnerable to the whims that rule politics and talk radio; or the public employee whose future depends, not on performance, but on the political profile that an ambitious minister happens to find electorally most useful. Think of the older person who is vulnerable to the culturally and institutionally unrestrained gang of youths in her area; or indeed of the young offender whose level of punishment depends on how far politicians or newspapers choose to whip up a culture of vengeance.

These examples illustrate what I describe as domination (Pettit 1997; Lovett forthcoming). In each case the people who suffer are subject to the interference of others; they are susceptible to the exercise of force by others, or the coercive threat of a penalty, or manipulation of their choices. They may not actually suffer interference at the hands of those who dominate them. What ensures that they are dominated is the fact that those others have the power of interfering with them in an arbitrary way—that is, in a way that they themselves do not control (for this formulation see Pettit 2008f). Individuals or groups dominate an agent just to the extent that they have such a power of interfering as they will. They are in a position to recognize the opportunities for interference and they do not face effective obstacles or deterrent costs that would make interference irrational—they can interfere with relative impunity.

I mention these instances of domination because if you concentrate your mind for a moment on what the experience of such subjection is like, and if you let yourself imagine or remember the bitter taste of such exposure to the power of another, then you will put yourself in a good position to understand the core idea in republicanism. For the central theme in republican concerns throughout the ages—the theme that explains all their other commitments—has been a desire to arrange things so that citizens are not exposed to domination of this kind.

Traditional republicans recognized two sorts of power or mastery that could induce domination, turning you into something like a slave or servant or subject and inducing the ingratiating mentality that they associated with such lack of standing. The one is the private power of other persons or groups, which the Romans called *dominium*; this is the sort of domination illustrated in the examples given. The other is the public power of the state itself, a power that they described as *imperium*. What they looked for was a dispensation of public power—a pattern of government—that would guard people against the private power of others, and so against domination by others, but would not itself become a dominating power in their lives: it would not have the aspect of a master (Kriegel 1995).

FREEDOM AS NONDOMINATION

To be against domination, however, may not seem to be the same as to be in favor of freedom. So why does the republican tradition equate freedom with the absence of domination? Freedom is normally equated with the absence of actual interference—the absence of force or coercion or manipulation and the like—and it may seem dishonest to present freedom instead as the absence of domination; that is, as the absence of a power of interference—

in particular, arbitrary or uncontrolled interference—on the part of others.

A little thought shows why it is entirely natural, however, and indeed totally traditional, to take freedom to require nondomination. If I am a fully free person, it must not be the case that I am subject to the arbitrary or uncontrolled will of others, at least in those basic domains of choice that can be made available to everyone in a society and are essential for a normal human life: that is, in the basic liberties (Pettit 2008a). Such freedom allows me to be influenced by other people in making my choices: others may deliberate with me about what I should do, even give me information about how they are willing to reward this or that option, but still leave it up to me to make my own decision. What freedom rules out is not that I am subject to such deliberative or related influence, but that I am subject to the will of others in a way that alienates my own control over my choices.

I will have control over what I choose in a given choice between options x, y, and z insofar as I can exercise my reason on the basis of the information available in selecting either x, or y, or z. Other people will alienate that control if, without my license, they remove one of those options, say by forcibly blocking me from taking it; or they replace one of the options, say by burdening the choice of the option with a penalty (or a nonrefusable reward); or they manipulate me by warping my capacity for reasoned choice or by giving me misleading information. In each of these cases they will exercise a degree of alien control over what I do. They will do so effectively to the extent that I am not defiant or countersuggestible and their initiative makes it more probable—more probable but not necessarily certain—that I will act to their taste.

Almost everyone will agree that freedom is reasonably described as the condition in which I avoid the alien control of others, particularly in the basic domains of human choice. The view that freedom is equivalent to the absence of active interference derives from the assumption that alien control is present just when there is active interference: say, when others actively resort to force or coercion or manipulation. But this assumption is false. I may be subject to the alien control of others without their actually interfering with me; if I think that the absence of interference in such a case means the presence of freedom, then I am deluded.

Consider first of all how active interference can mediate alien control. Others may interfere with me in a variety of ways, as we saw: they may manipulate me by undermining my capacity to make a reasoned choice or by denying me crucial information; they may exercise force, removing one or more options from the domain of choice; or they may practice coercion, replacing one or more options by penalized substitutes. Such interference will mediate alien control—the imposition of an alien will—provided that it is not subject to my ultimate say-so and control. That is to say, it is not like the interference of Ulysses' sailors in keeping him tied to the mast or the interference that my partner may practice, at my request, when she hides the chocolate or the cigars. So long as the interference is uncontrolled—so long as it is in that sense an arbitrary form of interference—it will subject me to a degree of alien control on the part of others and will reduce my freedom in the affected choices.

But uncontrolled or arbitrary interference is not the only means whereby others may alienate control of what I do in this or that situation. Take the scenario where others do not interfere in a given case because, as it happens, they are happy with the way I am acting or they are happy, at least for the moment, to let me have my way. They are able to interfere arbitrarily with me, should that be to their taste, and the only reason they do not interfere in a particular case is that I display a congenial profile. They leave me alone so long as I behave to their taste but they are ready to interfere if I ever begin to deviate from that pattern, or if their taste changes. They economize on interference, resorting to it only on a need-for-action basis.

Whether or not they resort to active interference, the agents in this scenario will enjoy a measure of control over all of the choices on my part that they are in a position to affect. They will exercise such control, partial or total, by monitoring or invigilating my behavior and being ready to interfere if interference is required to impose their taste. Whatever I do in the area of their control, I will do by their implicit leave. In the words of the old republican complaint, I will act in the area of their control only *cum permissu*: only with permission. For every option in any affected choice, to put the point in other terms, that option will have been replaced by a provisoed counterpart: I will no longer have access to the option *x*, for example, but only to *x*-provided-it-is-to-the-taste-of-those-others. In the domain of their control, I will live *in potestate domini*, and not *sui juris*: in the power of a master, not under my own jurisdiction.

If others have the power of arbitrarily interfering in certain of my choices, then they may exercise that power in either of two ways, alienating my own control in some measure. They may actively interfere in what I do, whether by force or coercion or manipulation, or they may invigilate what I do, exercising interference only when necessary. Either form of conduct will be a way of imposing their will on me and will make it more likely, defiance apart, that I act to their taste.

But interference and invigilation are not the only ways in which others may exercise alien control over what I do. They may make it obvious that they have a capacity to interfere arbitrarily in some choices and that they are invigilating what I do. In that case they will be able to give a boost to the effect of interference or invigilation: they will intimidate me, leading me to see that they have replaced any option *x* that I confront by the option *x*-provided-it-is-to-their-taste. Thus they will make it more likely still, defiance apart, that I will choose to their taste, or at least to what I take to be their taste. They will be able to rely on me to second-guess their wishes and to act accordingly. They will be employing their presumptive capacity to interfere arbitrarily in my choices in order to assert an alien control. But they will be employing it without having to exercise it in interference or to contemplate it in invigilation: I will do most of the work required to give their will a presence in my behavior.

We know that there may be invigilation without interference and we should also notice that there may be intimidation without invigilation or interference. This will materialize when others do not have the alleged capacity to interfere that they purport to make obvious, or do not display the associated exercise of invigilation, but are capable of misleading me on those counts: they can make me believe that they have the alleged capacity and are conducting the associated invigilation. Thus, even in the absence of the advertised power of interference or exercise of invigilation, they may intimidate me in just the same way as in the more straightforward case.[1]

The republican tradition has often focused on the situation where the dominated are aware of the control exercised by others over their lives, or are at least persuaded of such control—in which case the others have control of another kind—and consequently adopt the servile posture associated with intimidation; they censor the options that the powerful may dislike or they ingratiate themselves with the powerful in order to make such options more appealing (Pettit 2008d). The focus has given rise to a rich vocabulary of derision in which the dominated are said to have to kowtow or bend the knee to the powerful, to be obliged to fawn on them and curry their favor, to live at their mercy and beg their grace and favor. The republican lesson is that free persons, in contrast, can speak their minds, walk tall among their fellows, and look others squarely in the eye. They can command respect from those with whom they deal, not being subject to their arbitrary interference.

Two Faces of Freedom as Nondomination

The line of thought that I have been sketching shows that there are two ways in which the standard equation of freedom with noninterference goes wrong. First of all it makes the mistake of thinking that interference always mediates alien control and reduces freedom; it is guilty of what we might describe as the interference-always fallacy. This mistake comes of a failure to recognize that interference may be controlled by the person interfered with, as when my partner hides the chocolate or cigars at my bidding, and that when it is nonarbitrary in that sense it does not mediate the alien control of another and does not reduce my freedom.

The second mistake in the standard approach may be described, in parallel, as the interference-only fallacy. This consists in the thought that only interference can mediate the alien control of another and so only interference can have the effect of reducing freedom. This thought is mistaken because, as we have seen, others may impose their will on me, exercising an alien control, just by resort to invigilation or intimidation; they need not interfere in order to reduce my freedom.

In insisting that freedom requires nondomination, not noninterference, the republican tradition avoids both of these mistakes. Others will dominate me, as we saw, when they are in a position to interfere arbitrarily in certain choices. Such domination need not always occur in the presence of interference, or a power of interference, since the interference need not be arbitrary; it may be subject to my ultimate control. And such domination does not occur only as a result of active, arbitrary interference; it may also materialize by grace of invigilation or intimidation. Active interference is one way in which dominators may exploit the position of being able to interfere arbitrarily in my choices, using that position to alienate my control. Invigilation and intimidation represent other, less salient ways in which they may achieve that same effect.

Republican freedom is more demanding, then, than freedom in the contemporary sense of noninterference. It is true that controlled or nonarbitrary interference by another will not reduce my freedom in any choice. But the mere accessibility of uncontrolled interference to others—their being in a position where they have the knowledge and resources to practice such interference—will reduce my freedom. It will mean that I live partly under their control, and so not entirely under my own. I may be lucky and find that the more powerful have a taste for allowing me to act as I actually want to act or even a taste for letting me have my way. But whatever my fortune in that respect, I will still live in the shadow of another's power, whether the other be in the position of an employer, a spouse or a local bully.

According to the republican way of thinking I will not be a free person to the extent that I am exposed to such control in the exercise of the basic liberties; and I will suffer that loss of freedom even before any actual interference occurs. Freedom requires the sort of immunity to interference that would enable me to look every other person in the eye. I cannot count as free and yet be required to keep a weather eye open for the whims of the powerful, adopting a servile attitude toward them.

THE LONG TRADITION

The themes just rehearsed have a long history. Republicanism was kindled in classical Rome, where Cicero and other thinkers gloried in the vaunted independence and nondomination of the Roman citizen. Following Polybius, a Greek writer who championed the virtues of their constitution, they argued that, while the Roman republic gave its citizens the means and status whereby they could enjoy freedom as nondomination (this, of course, was only a half-truth) it did not itself represent a dominating presence in their life. Exemplifying a mixed constitution, so-called, the republic established strict rules under which power would be shared among many individuals and bodies in a regime of checks and balances, and what was done by the state had to be done in public, subject to the vigilance (and the considerable voting power) of a contestatory citizenry.

The Roman model served to highlight three republican themes for later generations. One was the personal ideal of freedom as nondomination and the others the associated institutional ideals of a mixed constitution and a contestatory citizenry. These ideas ignited enthusiasm among the burghers of Italian cities like Venice and Florence in the middle ages. They took pride in that, ruling themselves in a broadly republican manner, they did not have to beg anyone's favor in private or in public life. They were equal citizens of a common republic, and were of a different political species from the cowed subjects of papal Rome or courtly France.

The republican flame passed to the English-speaking world in the seventeenth century when the "commonwealth" tradition, which was forged in the experience of the English Civil War, established and institutionalized the view that king and people each lived under the discipline of the same law. Monarchy did not have to be done away with, in this version of republicanism, but it had to be made part of a constitutional order, and not allowed to become a center of absolute power. Enthusiasts for the idea of a commonwealth—an English word for "republic"—argued that, being protected by a fair law, no Briton had to depend on the arbitrary will of another, even the arbitrary will of the king; unlike the subjects of absolute monarchs, Britons were a race of sturdy and independent freemen.

This argument rebounded, of course, on Britain's own fortunes. For in the eighteenth century their American colonists became persuaded that they themselves were denied their due freedom: they had to depend on the arbitrary will of a foreign parliament. Perhaps they had to pay only one penny in taxes to the London government, as a contemporary writer put it, but the government that took that one penny had the power to take also their last penny (Priestley 1993, 140). Perhaps their British master was kindly and well disposed, but the subjects of a kindly master were subjects still; they did not have the immunity to arbitrary power that true freedom requires. The American colonists sought to escape British domination by severing their ties with the home country and by establishing, under a variant on the mixed constitution, the world's first large, self-described republic.

The American precedent, and indeed the British model of a constitutional monarchy, helped to foster the creation in the 1790s of the French republic. This second great revolution led, notoriously, to a reign of terror but it was born of the same desire to free ordinary people from subjugation to their would-be betters. Freedom as nondomination, as the French tradition spelled it out, required equality and indeed fraternity. It required a scenario in which they could each walk tall, secure in the knowledge that no one could lord it over them. Each could look others in the eye, seeing a fellow citizen there, and not anyone possessed of special privileges. No one had to fawn or toady, no one had to depend on the grace or favor of another.

But though the signal themes of the French Revolution were similar to those in the American War of Independence, they came to be articulated in an unfortunate manner. Under the influence of the idea that every state had to have a single sovereign ruler—this derived from the sixteenth-century jurist Jean Bodin (1992)—the French tradition followed Jean Jacques Rousseau in casting the republican sovereign as the people: ideally, the people as they participated in government; in practice, the people as they were electorally represented. The cult of sovereignty undermined the ideal of the mixed constitution in which different authorities would check and balance one another without any having absolute authority, and it also put the ideal of a contestatory citizenry in question. If the people as a whole were the sovereign authority, why would individual members have to keep an eye on its doings? These developments gave rise to the Franco-Prussian tradition of republican thought, represented in Rousseau and Kant, as distinct from the original Mediterranean-Atlantic tradition. Indeed, the sovereigntist commitments of these thinkers may even have led to the betrayal of the idea of freedom as nondomination. For while that idea certainly had a place in the emergence of the revolution—and, on a proper reading, in the work of Rousseau himself (Spitz 1995)—the new way of thinking must have encouraged the thought that freedom consists in active participation within a self-determining community.

That communitarian misreading of republican freedom, however, was only to come later. Whether in classical Rome, renaissance Italy, seventeenth-century England, or eighteenth-century America and France, all republicans saw domination as the great evil to be avoided in organizing a community and a polity. They thought of freedom as the supreme political value and equated it with not being stood over by anyone, even a benevolent and protective despot. To enjoy republican freedom was to be able to hold your head on high, to look others squarely in the eye, and to relate to your fellows without fear or deference.

THE RETREAT FROM REPUBLICAN FREEDOM

But if the republican way of defining freedom goes back to the beginnings of European civilization and has the merits for which I have argued, how did it ever go into decline? I shall argue that it went into decline, at least in part, because it came to be seen as too radical in character. This is a paradoxical claim, given that the idea of freedom as nondomination had been in the ascendant for nearly two millennia. But to my eye it is nonetheless plausible, even persuasive.

The shift to thinking of freedom as a matter of noninterference rather than nondomination began with the seventeenth-century, highly illiberal thinker Thomas Hobbes, but did not really catch on at the time (Pettit 2008e, chap. 7; Skinner 2008). It appeared again in the late eighteenth century, however, among thinkers who inspired the family of philosophies that came to be described as liberalism, in a term derived from the Spanish word *liberales*, as it was used of a progressive group in Cadiz in 1812. This time the shift took off with resounding success. The main figures responsible were the utilitarian thinker Jeremy Bentham and his very influential follower William Paley.

Writing in the wake of the enlightenment, in the age of Rousseau and Hume and Kant, Bentham and Paley took it for granted that the state had to care, not just about the freedom of the propertied males who had been the only target of concern up to then, but also about the freedom of women and workers. But if freedom meant nondomination, then a state that worked for the liberation of women and workers would have to turn the existing order upside down. Since the law of the time reduced women and servants to a status close to slavery, such a state would have to reject family law and master-servant law out of hand and establish a revolutionary order in its place. Bentham and Paley were reformers, not revolutionaries, and they shrank from endorsing a project for enabling all citizens, men and women, rich and poor, to live independently of the power of others. At the same time that they expanded the compass of the state's concern for freedom, then, they diluted the demands of the ideal, articulating them as demands for noninterference, not nondomination.

The retreat from republican liberty appears clearly in a book that Paley published in 1785 and that remained a best-selling text for well over a century. He agreed that something close to the conception of freedom as nondomination is favored in "the usage of common discourse"; according to this conception, as he said, freedom requires not just the absence of interference—or at least of interference that is "useless and noxious"—but the absence of even a "danger" of such interference (Paley 1825, 164–65). But he himself favored a rival conception in which, roughly, the absence of interference is enough on its own for freedom; just the danger of interference—just the accessibility of interference to others—does not make a person unfree.

Paley has a number of complaints against the established, republican conception of freedom, among them the spurious claim that there is a danger of interference to the extent to which there is a probability of interference, and that the accessibility of interference to a benevolent despot would not make for a danger in the relevant, probabilistic sense (Pettit 2008d). But his main argument is that the ideal of freedom as nondomination is socially too radical. Let the state proclaim freedom as nondomination as an ideal for the whole citizenry, not just for propertied males, and it will not be able to deliver what it promises. Such an ideal of freedom, he wrote, would be "unattainable in experience," would "inflame expectations that can never be gratified," and would "disturb the public content with complaints, which no wisdom or benevolence of government can remove" (Paley 1825, 168).

Paley opted for a view of freedom as the absence of interference, or at least the absence of "noxious and useless" interference, because it does not hold out the specter of such radical utopianism. He argued that, while the state ought to promote the probability of noninterference, it should not worry about the fact that some people live under the power of others. If those others are benevolent, or are capable of being ingratiated at little cost, then such subjection will not compromise people's freedom as noninterference. Thus, if women live under the power of men, or workers under the power of masters, that will not affect their freedom as noninterference, so long as the men or the masters do not actually interfere with them; they do not throw their weight about. Paley did not explicitly address the case of women and workers but he showed his colors in the claim that people's freedom as a whole might even be better served under "the edicts of a despotic prince," rather than under "the resolutions of a popular assembly," were that prince sufficiently benevolent (Paley 1825, 166). This claim would be anathema to any republican, since even a benevolent despotic prince would have a power of interfering at will and with impunity in his subject's lives; he would enjoy alien control over them and be in that sense a danger to them.

In putting forward his argument for freedom as noninterference, Paley was conscious of employing a new way of thinking about freedom, as is shown by his admission that the conception of freedom as nondomination was favored in "the usage of common discourse." The rival conception of noninterference had been in circulation from the mid 1770s and the young Jeremy Bentham had no doubt but that he was the author of the idea. Thus he claimed in a letter of the time that it was a "discovery I had made, that the idea of liberty, imported nothing in it that was positive: that it was merely a negative one"; under this account, he said, freedom amounted consisted simply in "the absence of restraint" (Long 1977, 54).

The triumph of the new way of thinking about freedom may have been aided by a second development, associated with the French political thinker Benjamin Constant. In 1819 he delivered a lecture on the liberty of the ancients and the moderns, as he put it, to a club in Paris. This had an enormous impact on his contemporaries and successors. Indeed its influence can be seen in the repetition of its fundamental theme in Isaiah Berlin's (1958) lecture, 140 years later, on "'Two Concepts of Liberty."

Constant cast the traditional republican way of thinking in communitarian terms and presented freedom as noninterference—or at least something that came to be interpreted in that way—as the only alternative. On this reading the ancient tradition had looked for a freedom that consists in having a small say in how things are done in the public sphere, by virtue of participation in collective decision-making. By contrast, the modern conception, according to Constant, takes freedom to consist in having a large, even exclusive, say in how things are done in private. This communitarian casting of the traditional, republican way of thinking about freedom may have made it attractive to romantics, and may have become part of the Franco-Prussian version of republicanism, but it effectively transformed it into a utopian ideal, suitable only for small city-states. As the communitarian construction of republican freedom became widely accepted, it eclipsed the notion of freedom as nondomination and made freedom as noninterference look like the only realistic alternative.

Through the efforts of people like Bentham and Paley, the new conception of freedom as noninterference rapidly gained sway. It was made into the supreme political value by classical liberals of the early nineteenth century, the forerunners of today's right-wing libertarians; and it was generally respected in the work of more left-wing liberals too. They tended to treat it as an important value but, recognizing that its demands did not go very far—recognizing perhaps that it was consistent with some people having great power over others—they argued for the political importance of other values like equality or justice or utility.

We can still see the traces of this pattern in the work of contemporary left-of-center liberals. Thus John Rawls (1971) argued for the importance of equal liberty in something close to the sense of liberty as noninterference, and then in addition for the importance of economic and social equality; famously, he urged that the state should tolerate only those inequalities that serve indirectly to improve the lot of the worst-off members of society. And in a parallel attempt to supplement freedom as noninterference, Philippe Van Parijs (1995) argued that the we should be concerned not just about the interference of others in people's lives—not just about formal freedom—but also about the natural and social obstacles that prevent people from enjoying the noninterference that the law protects: we should be seek to make such formal freedom real or effective (for a critique, see Pettit 2001, chap. 6).

SOCIALISM AND FEMINISM

Although the notion of freedom as nondomination went into serious retreat under the pressure of the rival idea, I should say that it did not disappear altogether. It remained influential in two areas: first, among those who campaigned for the cause of workers and, second, among those who upheld the cause of women.

One of the core ideas in nineteenth-century workers' movements, whether of a Marxist or a social democratic character, was that of wage slavery: the idea that those who labored in the new manufacturing industries were slaves insofar as they were exposed to the arbitrary power of masters who could fire them at will and ensure that they were not employed elsewhere. Victor Hugo's *Les Miserables* documented the predicament, but it was familiar to anyone who fought for the right of workers to organize in unions and establish a countervailing power to the power of their employers. The existence of uncontained employer power, not just its exercise, made workers into slaves, in this view of things. That socialist account of the predicament of laborers made sense only based on the republican conception of freedom as nondomination. Socialism was the offspring, in the industrial arena, of classical republicanism (Skinner 1998).

Socialism depended on the republican conception of freedom as nondomination in advancing the idea of wage slavery; in fact, that very formula had its origins in republican circles. Talk of wage slavery was minted in the early years of the American republic when the fear was raised that those employed in manufacture would be "wages-slaves" and would be exposed to "that haughty, overbearing disposition, that purse-proud insolence" of the industrial employer (Sandel 1996, 153, 172–74).

The socialist movement was not alone in invoking the republican conception of freedom. The feminist movement took a similar turn in arguing against what was sometimes called "white slavery" in the nineteenth century (Pateman 1988, 123); this was the counterpart to the wage slavery that socialists decried. The feminist complaint was that so long as women lived under the thumb of men, subject to their control, they would remain unfree. Their husbands might not exercise force or coercion or manipulation in active interference but they would still control how the women lived. And to the extent that men enjoyed such control, women lived in subjection and slavery.

The idea was well expressed in Ibsen's play *A Doll's House*. Nora is denied nothing but macaroons by her doting husband Thorvald, and even this restriction is a light burden, since she is able to hide the macaroons in her skirts. As Ibsen makes clear, however, her comfortable existence is entirely blighted by the unquestionable power that he has over her. The existence of that power is an evil in itself, even though the power is scarcely ever exercised. Nora is not *sui juris*: she does not live in her own jurisdiction but under the rule of her husband.

Although the socialist and feminist movements continued to draw on the republican idea of freedom as nondomination, however, they did not consciously do so. The general presumption in the nineteenth and twentieth centuries was that freedom means noninterference. This was cast as a negative conception of freedom, and the only alternative account that received any recognition was a positive conception of freedom as self-mastery; this was sometimes given a communitarian twist, with self-mastery being associated with membership in a self-governing community (Berlin 1958). The republican view is like the positive in focusing on mastery rather than interference and like the negative in requiring the absence of mastery by others rather than the presence of self-mastery. But it became entirely hidden in the formulas that dominated political thought and practice throughout the period.

REPUBLICANISM AND LIBERALISM

I mentioned earlier that in the old republican way of thinking about freedom there are two principal concerns. One is a worry about the danger represented by the private power of others, *dominium* and the other a worry about the danger represented by the public power of the state, *imperium*.

The first concern argues for having the state establish a social order under which, in the basic domains of individual choice, citizens are well protected against the arbitrary power of other citizens, of outsiders to their society, and of any groups that such individuals might form. Citizens, in the traditional way of thinking, were only mainstream, propertied males, but in any plausible revival of the approach they will include women as well as men, the poor as well as the propertied, the marginal as well as the mainstream.

The second concern argues for having a state that operates under civic control of government so that citizens are not unnecessarily exposed to an arbitrary power on the part of the state itself. On the one side, the conception of freedom as nondomination supports an ideal of social empowerment and protection and, on the other, an ideal of civic control over government.

These two concerns mean that republicanism is a demanding political philosophy—and particularly demanding once the citizenry is not restricted to an elite. The philosophy is socially radical insofar as it requires that the state should do everything possible to establish a social order in which individual citizens can enjoy independence and escape subjection to the arbitrary power of others. And it is politically radical insofar as it allows that the coercive interventions of the state—the interventions involved in imposing laws and taxes—will not themselves take away from people's freedom if they are subject to the checks that would make them nonarbitrary and nondominating.

On the social side, this approach to government gives the state a substantial and consequential task; it gives it broadly a social democratic agenda. The state is not just to be a night watchman who protects against internal and external turmoil but an agency that moulds and shapes society. On the political side, the approach allows the properly ordered state to act in pursuit of its agenda without infringing on people's freedom as nondomination. The interventions of the state may restrict the exercise of freedom in the way that natural obstacles do, and so there is reason to economize on state action, but if they are properly checked then they will not dominate the citizenry; however restrictive of individual choice, they will be the interventions of an agency that the people controls, not the impositions of an unchecked master. Thus the approach suggests a constitutional-democratic project of seeking out the restraints whereby the state can be made less arbitrary and dominating.

The implications of a republican or civicist philosophy differ dramatically in these two respects from the implications of a libertarian philosophy in which the only value recognized is that of freedom as noninterference. Libertarianism—right-wing liberalism—is conservative rather than radical on both the social and political fronts. The social conservatism derives from the interference-only fallacy embedded in the equation between freedom and noninterference, the political conservatism from the interference-always fallacy.

Libertarians are socially conservative insofar as they seek an order in which it is enough for freedom that people do not suffer active interference in the basic domains of human choice; by the interference-only principle, after all, active interference is the sole threat to freedom. The libertarian approach does not provide a ground for worrying about any imbalances of power that allow some people control over others, then, just so long as the imbalances do not issue in active interference. But libertarians are also politically conservative insofar as they acknowledge no difference in the ledger of freedom between the interference of the state in people's lives and the interference of criminal offenders; by the interference-always principle each intervention reduces the freedom of those affected. Since the state is inevitably a source of interference, then—as in coercive legislation, taxation, and punishment—it is essentially opposed to freedom; even when it acts to prevent interference it does so by perpetrating interference.

Paley's focus on obnoxious and useless interference, it is true, would allow the recognition of a difference between criminal and state interference, but Bentham and others did not endorse his perspective. For them, any form of interference is inimical to freedom, be it the interference of the thief or the taxman. "All coercive laws," according to Bentham (1843, 503), "are as far as they go abrogative of liberty." This position means that libertarians who make freedom as noninterference into the only political value—Bentham himself did not do this, of course—must be loathe to entrust the state with any substantial tasks. One libertarian line, for example, is to say that the state should be allowed to impose coercive legislation or taxation when and only when the interference thereby perpetrated is clearly justified by the interference it prevents.

The difference between the republican and libertarian approaches comes out nicely in the attitude they are likely to adopt on issues of welfare. The main issue in welfare policy is how far the state should go in drawing on the funds provided by taxation to insure the poor, and people more generally, against those forms of dependency that derive from inadequate resources, lack of education or information, medical need, and reduced access to justice. And on this issue the two philosophies are set up to go in quite different ways.

Libertarians who equate freedom with noninterference will think, first, that any state interventions involve coercive taxation, itself an instance of the very loss of liberty that should be prevented; and, second, that such interventions may not be required by liberty as noninterference, so far as dependency fails to trigger actual interference by others. Thus they will be able to make only a very uncertain connection between the promotion of freedom as noninterference in itself and the establishment of a welfare system. A line that attracts many libertarians is to say that, rather than having the state tax the rich to help out the poor, we should rely on the philanthropy of the rich to have this effect—we might even provide tax breaks to facilitate it—and insure people only against the most extreme cases of emergency.

The view that a republican perspective would support is very different (Pettit 2006). In this approach, the provision of welfare may count as essential for protecting people against dependency, and the consequent loss of republican liberty; it may be necessary, even when the dependency does not trigger active interference. That is the socially radical aspect of the doctrine. In this approach, furthermore, the taxation needed to support a social security system need not count as domination, and need not count therefore as a serious assault on people's liberty; it may represent a suitably controlled, and so nonarbitrary form of government interference. That reflects the politically radical side of the philosophy.

The republican perspective breaks with the libertarian, then, in two ways. It allows us to deny that the properly ordered welfare state takes from the freedom of those from whom it redistributes; it merely imposes limitations like those associated with natural obstacles. And it allows us to see the task of providing welfare as one that is essential for the freedom of those citizens favored by the redistribution. Unlike libertarianism, moreover, republicanism does not see philanthropy as an acceptable alternative to the welfare state. Those who depend on the charity of the wealthy are in no position to command respect and assume the status that goes with freedom as nondomination.

On welfare policy, the republican approach is likely to come much closer to left-wing liberalism than to the right-wing version associated with libertarianism. But that does not mean, of course, that the approach is really another version of left-wing liberalism. Unlike such liberalism, it has the signal merit of invoking just the single, engaging value of freedom as nondomination in arguing for state policies; in this respect, it offers a nice counterpart to libertarianism. And that single value offers us an effective criterion for resolving issues about how the state should be organized as well as about what the state should do; it gives us an ideal by which to evaluate the architecture of the state as well as its agenda.

THE CIVIC REPUBLICAN PROJECT

The civic republican project is to reverse the retreat from republican liberty that occurred in the late eighteenth century and to employ the conception of liberty as nondomination to rethink the form that the state should take as well as the policy agenda that the state should adopt (Lovett and Pettit 2009). The tradition gives us two guiding principles: first, a constitutional-democratic principle to the effect that the architecture of the state should be designed to ensure as far as possible that public power or *imperium* is not dominating; and, second, a social-democratic counterpart to that effect that the state should pursue an agenda of reducing to the greatest extent feasible the domination that goes with private power or *dominium*. The state should intervene so as to guard against private domination and should organize itself so as to guard against public domination. The civic republican project is to translate those principles into specific designs for the civic control of public power and into specific policies for the establishment of a social order in which even the poorest citizens can command the respect of their fellows, conscious of not being exposed to private power in the basic domains of human choice.

This project has considerable intellectual momentum, with many figures cooperating in associated tasks. In the past decade or so there have been numerous contributions. Apart from Pettit (1997) and Skinner (1998), there are broadly congenial accounts of the tradition in Oldfield (1990), Sellers (1995), Brugger (1999), Viroli (2002), Honohan (2002), and Maynor (2003). There are a number of collections of papers on the relevance of the approach for political and legal theory (Weinstock and Nadeau 2004; Honohan and Jennings 2006; Laborde and Maynor 2007; Besson and Martí 2008; White and Leighton 2008). There is a range of studies of issues raised by criminal justice, constitutionalism, democracy, international relations, multiculturalism, and social welfare in which the civic republican conception of freedom as nondomination, broadly understood, has been a guiding thread (Braithwaite and Pettit 1990; Richardson 2002; Slaughter 2005; Bellamy 2007; Bohman 2007; Raventós 2007; Laborde 2008).

Apart from these volumes, there has also been a large and increasing number of articles published on republican themes, both for and against, and a growing literature in other languages as well, in particular, French, Italian, and Spanish. The European interest in civic republicanism has been encouraged by a renewed interest in the historical origins of the classical republican tradition (Van Gelderen and Skinner 2002) and in its contemporary development and application (Spitz 2005; Bourdeau and Merrill 2007). It has been boosted, of course, by the fact that, after his election in 2004, the Spanish prime minister, José Luis Rodríguez Zapatero, explicitly adopted republicanism as a philosophy of his government (Pettit 2008a). There is more on this topic in the next chapter.

In the remainder of this chapter I will look briefly at the sorts of policies on these two fronts that civic republicanism is likely to support. First I consider the lessons of civic republicanism for the agenda of government and then its implications for governmental architecture.

Before taking up those tasks, however, it may be useful to add a word about an abstract, somewhat technical issue. I assume that the state should be organized architecturally, and should be orientated in its agenda, so that freedom as nondomination—or, if that amounts to something distinct, equal freedom as nondomination (Pettit 1997, chap. 4; Lovett 2001; and forthcoming)—is likely to be at a maximum. But in taking such an outcome-centered or consequentialist view of how the state should be judged within civic republicanism, I do not suggest that the state should have the sort of discretion that would enable its agents to deny one person's freedom in order to maximize freedom overall. There can be no freedom as nondomination unless people are more or less immune to such intrusions, even such benevolent intrusions, into their basic liberties. So the idea is that, while the rules of the system should be designed so as to maximize freedom as nondomination across an inclusive, equal citizenry, the agents of the state should be required to conform strictly to those rules (Rawls 1955).

Social Democracy: A Social Order to Guard against Private Power

Four basic sorts of initiative are required to guard against private power, along republican lines. The first is to firm up the infrastructure of nondomination, providing as far as possible for a resilient economy, a reliable rule of law, an inclusive knowledge system, a sound health system, and a sustainable environment. As many other values depend on the realization of such conditions for their capacity to flourish, the same is true of the value of freedom as nondomination. The second initiative that freedom as nondomination requires of the state, however, is that it empower the distinctively vulnerable, providing them with the resources of basic functioning, as Amartya Sen (1985) describes them. The third is that it provide protection for people in general, whether against internal or external enemies. And the fourth is that it regulate the powerful agents and agencies that, regardless of the other measures in place, still manage to exercise a certain alien control over ordinary citizens.

We need not go into detail here on the forms that initiatives in these areas might usefully take or on the questions that they raise. It is easier to expand on what the republican agenda requires in a specific institutional context and the next chapter, which reviews the performance of the Spanish government, provides an opportunity for doing this. There are three general points that might be usefully made at this more abstract stage of argument, however. One bears on the general means of protection available against domination, a second on the limitations of what can be said on a purely philosophical basis, and a third on the significance of international relations.

The first point is that there are many forms of protection against domination that a state might provide, and that institutional imagination is required to ensure that a variety of possibilities are put on the table for consideration. Take the issue of what protections should be put in place to empower the more vulnerable in relationships where there is a real prospect of domination, say, domestic or workplace relations. There are at least three different resources that the vulnerable should ideally be able to access if they are to be sufficiently protected in these situations: rights, powers, and options.

The vulnerable must be given rights that enable them to trigger the law against certain abuses, as in the right of workers to sue for wrongful dismissal or form a union, or the right of a woman to charge her husband with domestic violence or to seek separation or divorce. But those rights will be worth little or nothing unless the vulnerable operate in a culture where they have the powers required to assert or support the rights. Thus workers must be organized so that they have the effective power of collective bargaining, and women must be so supported in the community that they have the power of calling in the police against an abusive husband: they must not be subject to such shame, for example, that the right is meaningless. And apart from rights and powers, the vulnerable in such contexts must also, ideally, be provided with options of exit. Thus workers will be all the better protected against workplace domination if they have access to a reasonable state income, should they leave their employment. And women will be all the better protected against abusive partners if there are homes for battered women in which they can seek at least temporary refuge.

The second point to be made about policies for guarding against private domination is that the forms they take should be determined in good part by empirical experience of the effects of different policies; philosophy alone cannot dictate the best way of doing things. Should there be a universal health system or provision for universal insurance? Should there be a means-tested social security arrangement or something on the lines of the basic income proposal (Raventós 2007)? Should police forces be organized centrally or at local level or in a mix of both systems? Should the powerful be regulated by high marginal rates of taxation, as was more common in the middle of the last century, or by restrictions on what they may do with their money, or by incentives to use their money for public causes, or by a variety of such measures? All of these questions have to be resolved, not as a matter of abstract principle, but on the basis of empirical study.

The third general point about policies for guarding against private power is that strictly they include policies in the international as well as the domestic arena. This point is worth emphasizing since, for purely pragmatic reasons, we have little to say in the remainder of the book on issues of international relations. It provides the opportunity for outlining the republican ideal as it applies in this forum (Pettit 2009a, and forthcoming).

What order does the ideal of nondomination require among states, as states are more or less currently formed? Take those states that are themselves subject to such control by their own people that, if the state is dominated, then its people are dominated. Here the ideal suggests that states ought to be protected against the domination of other states and other state-sized bodies such as multinational companies, religious institutions, and other networks. They ought to be protected, not just against active intervention or interference on the part of those agencies, military, economic, or cultural, but also against exposure to a capacity for

uncontrolled intervention and against the invigilation and intimidation that this can impose. This demand for an international
order of nondomination—a republican law of peoples—is richer
than the traditional demand for nonintervention alone but it is
more austere, and more sensible, than the demand for a regime of
cosmopolitan justice in which every state has the same duties to all
individuals, citizens and noncitizens alike.

But if this is the ideal for well-ordered states that are controlled
by their peoples, what of states that are ill-ordered and disordered?
What of those states where control and power are in the hands of
an elite, and may be used oppressively against some other groups?
And what of those states that are so badly organized that they
cannot provide the basic services that are their reponsibility under
almost any political philosophy? In these cases, the ideal of nondomination imposes on the community of well-ordered states the
obligation to do everything that is possible to facilitate the formation of suitably popular states, provided the costs of what is done
count as intuitively proportional and reasonable. There is a lot to
be said on this issue but this is not a suitable context in which to
try to say it.

Given that these are the requirements of freedom as nondomination in the international arena, how are they to be fulfilled?
Well-ordered states in general will have to establish institutional
means, a common international discourse, and an international
legal order, on the basis of which to regulate their relations with
one another, to identify nondominating resolutions of their difficulties, and to provide as well as possible for human beings who
live in states that cannot serve their citizens properly or that actually practice abuses against them. There will have to be a network
of international agencies that are powerful enough to act on these
fronts but restricted enough, under a regime of international law,
not to be dominating in relation to the states and peoples who
uphold it.

But it may be said, quite reasonably, that this is not likely to
provide much protection for weaker states, since the agencies will
often be shaped by the more powerful and they are unlikely to
guard, for example, against domination of an economic sort. Here

the remedy may have to involve regional or related forms of collaboration among states, not the international variety considered
so far. Those weaker states with common vulnerabilities will have
to unite in common cause against more powerful states, or against
bodies like multinational corporations, and use the power that
they thereby gain to guard themselves against domination. At this
level they can protect themselves only by linking their fortunes
with one another. Or so at any rate it seems; the matter clearly calls
for more research and reflection.

Constitutional Democracy: A Civic Order to Guard against Public Power

One of the most questionable assumptions in what we have argued
so far may be the claim that government can operate in a society in
such a way that, while it imposes coercive legislation and taxation,
it does not itself dominate people. It puts restrictions into place
that affect their choices but these restrictions, like the limitations
imposed by natural obstacles, need not represent the controlling
will of an uncontrolled agency in their lives. They will be nonarbitrary insofar as they are controlled by the very people affected.
They will be nonarbitrary in roughly the way in which the actions
of Ulysses' sailors, or the actions of my partner in hiding the cigars
and chocolate, are nonarbitrary. They are intrusions that answer
to the bidding of those on whom they intrude.

The claim that government can be nonarbitrary and the state
nondominating is going to make sense only if we acknowledge
certain natural and historical necessities. These have always been
acknowledged in a realistic way by the main streams of republican
thought, although they are rejected in utopian strands of state-of-
nature thinking. The first necessity is that we are all are born into
an ongoing society; the second that ours is a world in which there
is no effective possibility of living out of society; and the third that
every society has to organize its business centrally and coercively.
These facts do not testify in themselves to any domination by others. It is not as if it is because of the controlling presence of certain

powers in our lives that we are forced to live in society, under a collective regime. We live, as by a natural and historical necessity, under these constraints; they are as inescapable as gravity.

When will a government be dominating, then, and when nondominating? Government will dominate any citizen if its initiatives are not controlled by the citizenry as a whole—the people—or if that citizen does not have an equal share in such civic or popular control. Government will be nondominating for a citizen if its initiatives are subject to popular control and if that citizen enjoys equality with others in the exercise of that control. Government as such is a natural necessity in this picture. It will be nonarbitrary in relation to me, a randomly chosen citizen—it will be subject to my control in the highest feasible degree—insofar as the people as a whole control what is done and I play an equal part in the exercise of that collective control. In a slogan, the nondominating government will be the government that is subject to the effective and equally shared control of the people or citizenry.

Is it unrealistic to expect that people might be able to play an equal part in the exercise of collective control over government, given the different levels of political activism across a society? Not necessarily, for reasons that appeared in another context, when we saw that I may have invigilatory control over someone without actually exercising active interference. I will have such control insofar as I stand by, able and willing to interfere if that is necessary in order to get the person to behave to my taste. In the same way I will share equally in the collective control of government if I have an equal opportunity with others to assume an active role, electoral or otherwise, in shaping what government does. Even when I do not assume such a role, my inaction represents a contribution to the collective direction of government. My inaction may be prompted by laziness rather than acceptance, of course, but that is my personal failure, not a failure of the system. The system may reasonably be required to provide me with the knowledge and opportunity for political action but it cannot be faulted, and cannot be held to be dominating, just because I am too lazy to be active myself.

This account of what is required to make government interference nonarbitrary and nondominating supports a number of immediate implications. The first is that the nondominating government will have to be democratic in the basic, etymological sense of the word. It will have to be a government that is subject to the *kratos* or power of the *demos* or people—as we may assume, the equally shared power of the people. But what does democracy in this basic, republican sense require? A second and third implication of the account given shed some light on that question.

The second implication is that the citizenry may exercise effective and equal control over government, and be in that sense a democratic people, even when the governing individuals or body are distinct from the people themselves. That I control what is done by someone does not require that I am that very person; and that a people controls how government acts does not require that it is the governing agency. That government is subject to effective and equal popular control does not entail, then, that it has to be exercised by the people themselves, as in Rousseau's image of the self-governing assembly. Rousseau made a break with the Mediterranean-Atlantic tradition of republicanism in giving such exclusive importance to the idea of the sovereign, participatory assembly.

But the conception of nondominating government also has a third implication, bearing on electoral rather than participatory democracy. The fact that those in government are controlled effectively and equally by the people does not entail that they are elected; nor does the fact that they are elected mean that they are popularly controlled. That certain officials are appointed by elected authorities, for example, or even that they inherit office, as in the case of the constitutional monarch, does not mean that they are uncontrolled; they may be subject to checks and balances that put them under an effective popular discipline and may count as authorized representatives of the people (Pettit 2009b). And, on the other side, the fact that certain authorities are elected does not guarantee that they are subject to popular control. Let someone not care about being reelected, and the fact that they came to office via election may have no controlling effect on their actions. This has always been recognized in mainstream republicanism, as when James Madison (1987), one of the founders of the American republic, warned against the problem of an "elective despotism."

So what does the effective and equal control of government by the people require? What does democracy in the republican sense entail? The answer comes at two levels, one conceptual, the other institutional.

Conceptually, republican democracy requires that government should be directed by the egalitarian expression of common concerns, never by sectional interests. Common concerns will be ones that each member of the society is disposed to avow as interests that are relevant to determining what should be done in the name of the people as a whole; if you like, they are perceptible common interests. Different concerns may be differently weighted by different individuals but everyone will acknowledge them as interests that are appropriately put in play when determining what the government ought to do.

Common concerns in this sense contrast with considerations to do with what is good for one particular subgroup (and perhaps bad for another), or with what is good for the community as a whole according to a view that not everyone shares. They need not be private interests that all in the society happen to share independently, as when all happen to have an interest in seeing a particular sport or a particular religion promoted; they may not even be parallel private interests, as in the interest that each has in his or her own health or prosperity. They will mostly be interests of the community as a whole that all members can recognize as having a certain importance, at least if they are prepared to live on equal terms with others. Examples might be that the community be peaceful and cohesive, that it allow individuals to live their own lives without excessive public direction, that it provide a safety net for those in emergency need, that it look after the victims of local, natural catastrophes, that it establish rules for private and public ownership, and of course that it have governing structures that make it possible for decisions between policies that can equally claim to be faithful to common concerns to be resolved—to be resolved, in particular, according to procedures that themselves fit with common concerns.

The conceptual connection between the government that is effectively and equally controlled by the people and a government of common concerns is recognized in the republican tradition in the recurrent theme that government ought to be directed to the common good: as I understand it, the perceptible common good. But the tradition tends to take that conceptual connection for granted and to focus more on the question of what a republican democracy requires in the way of governing institutions. What institutions are required in order to ensure, as far as possible, that government is subject to the appropriate form of popular control: that it is directed by the egalitarian expression of common concerns?

Institutionally, according to the mainline tradition, the effective, equal control of government requires that government should operate under the mixed constitution in a context of civic invigilation. The ideas of the mixed constitution and the contestatory citizenry were dropped in the Franco-Prussian tradition, as we saw earlier, in favor of a centralism that Napoleon established as the norm. But elsewhere they remain a centerpiece of republican thought and practice. While they are highly schematic ideas, and allow of various interpretations, they retain a place in almost every articulation of the Mediterranean-Atlantic version of the republican approach.

How reliable and useful is the tradition in directing us to these twin devices? The question may be most usefully addressed by looking at how far they figure in the way that voluntary associations organize their affairs democratically. Take the condominium in which the owners of different apartments in a building or complex have to incorporate so as to conduct common business. These co-owners will want to exercise effective, equal control over the actions of their body, ensuring that the initiatives adopted are directed by the egalitarian expression of common concerns, and not by any more special interests. So how do they do this?

The concerns that the owners will want to satisfy are fairly obvious. They will want to create a body that can deal reasonably with each of them individually, and indeed with outside persons: it must be able to avow coherent principles and propositions, respond appropriately to new information and opportunity, and act as a consistent, intelligible, and reliable center of agency. They will want a body that treats each of them equally and that does not intrude too much into their private affairs; it may be able to dictate how the outside of the building is painted but not how each apartment is internally furnished. And they will want a body that is financially responsible, astute in its dealings with outside agencies, and able to establish a civil culture among residents.

How are members of the condominium likely to control the pursuit of their common affairs—their government, if you like—so that such concerns, and such concerns only, will be paramount in the decisions taken and the policies implemented? In order to do their business effectively, the members of the condominium will certainly want to elect a committee to do the job; they will not be able to do the job in a committee-of-the-whole. But they will not want to give this committee a carte blanche, since otherwise it might act in its own individual interests, not in the interests of the membership at large. The owners will want to subject committee members to the prospect of periodic reelection, they will want this election to be competitive so that the performance of committee members can be challenged, and they will want the election to be conducted on the basis of something like one owner, one vote. Nor, in all likelihood, will they be content with purely electoral constraints. They will also try to ensure that those who are authorized to act in the corporate name are subject to a battery of nonelectoral checks.

The nonelectoral constraints that are likely to appeal to a condominium will include examples like the following, and may well be encoded in a written constitution.

- *Rule-of-law constraints* on committee decisions, ensuring that the committee can act only on the basis of established principles that apply to all and do not discriminate against any individual or group
- *Private-right constraints* that block the committee from taking actions that would intrude on the affairs of individual owners, say by requiring them to furnish the interiors of their apartments in a certain pattern
- *Invigilation constraints* that require the committee to publicize its decisions or plans, and its reasons for supporting them, inviting public discussion and challenge and establishing means for having objections heard and adjudicated

- *Separation-of-power constraints* that subject committee proceedings to the checking of other bodies, say, an oversight "senate," and that require bodies that adjudicate objections to be independent of the committee
- *Regulatory constraints* that subject the committee to monitoring by independent officials or bodies, appointed from among owners or from outside, such as auditors or solicitors
- *Outsourcing constraints* that require the committee to outsource decisions to an independent arbitrator or advisor in areas where rival, individual interests are engaged
- *Tie-breaking constraints* that ensure that decisions between equally acceptable policies are not indefinitely delayed and are made by procedures that themselves fit with common concerns: depending on the case, these might authorize a committee vote, or a referendum, or referral to an expert or impartial body
- *Amendment constraints* that make it possible to alter electoral arrangements or any of the constraints on this list—including the amendment constraints themselves—but only in a certain manner, say, by a supermajoritarian support in a committee-of-the-whole

The sorts of institutions that a condominium would be inclined to put in place answer, very broadly, to the idea of the mixed constitution, and they incorporate a role for a contestatory membership. There are many agents and agencies involved under this picture in the governance of the group. They include the representatives on the committee, the members who elect them, the members who raise objections to committee proposals, the professional auditors or attorneys who question committee procedures, the bodies formed to adjudicate such objections and questions, and the committee-of-the-whole. Those different agents have to follow set constitutional guidelines that identify the tasks to pursue and the best mode of pursuing them, if the condominium is to constitute a unified body. And they are forced to operate in an interactive, involved manner, providing a check and balance on one another's initiatives under the critical, vigilant gaze of members. The condominium emerges from a swirl of activity among the members, but the swirl is institutionally designed to generate a coherent pattern of activity, and a pattern that respects the common concerns of members.

In giving life after this pattern to a mixed constitution and a contestatory membership, the condominium shows what it might mean for a regime to be a government of common concerns and, more specifically, a government that is directed by the egalitarian expression of common concerns. Every member of the condominium is in a position to contest plans formed on the basis of uncontested reasons or to contest those very reasons themselves. And things are designed so that this permanent possibility of contestation, reinforced by the system of mutual checks and balances, means that the concerns that prevail in decision-making, whether decision-making over options or over procedures for breaking tied options, are ones that count as common to all.

The example of the condominium points us to the sorts of institutions that republican theory is likely to support in order to promote the effective and equal popular control of government, ensuring that common concerns are given center stage and sectional concerns are sidelined. I shall not dwell in detail on how the institutions might be developed except to comment that in a large-scale society there will be a much greater need for discussion and contestation in order to identify evolving common concerns and to keep government faithful to them. The swirl of civic and political, judicial, and bureaucratic activity that is going to be required to give life to a coherent democratic polity is of a different order again from that required by a simple body like a condominium.

Is it utopian to expect that an advanced, multicultural society will be able to develop a sense of common concerns of the kind that the argument presupposes? I do not think so. In any inclusively democratic society, there will be continual discussion and disagreement about what government should be doing in this area or that. This may materialize in the home, in the workplace, in cafes and bars, or in consultative or contestatory forums, in parliament or on the media. Such democratic discussion will not generally run into the ground, with the different sides unable to muster considerations in defense of their proposals that they can expect the others to acknowledge as relevant (if not persuasive) arguments. The very process of deliberation, even deliberation that does not lead to consensus, will generate an evolving sense of the considerations that are relevant or irrelevant to determining the policies of government. Those considerations will then point us toward a body of common concerns that people each recognize as pertinent to public decisions, even as they diverge on the precise weightings that different considerations should be given.

Public deliberation and dialogue, public contestation and challenge, thus play a crucial role in this republican story about how government should be popularly controlled (Martí 2006). The doctrine of the mixed constitution does not look just to the cogs and wheels of established law for the control of government. As the doctrine is understood here, the people have to be a restless, engaged and critical body—certainly the different social movements they support have to have this character—if there is to be any hope of keeping government in check and ensuring that it is not an arbitrary presence in their lives. An eighteenth-century Scot, Adam Ferguson (1767, 167), put the point well when he said that good government cannot be secured by law and constitution alone; it relies crucially on "the refractory and turbulent zeal" of an engaged people.

CONCLUSION

It may be useful, in conclusion, to sum up the main points in this overview.

1. Republicanism in its original Mediterranean-Atlantic version invokes the ideal of freedom as nondomination as a basis for identifying the architecture that the state should display and the agenda it should further. It contrasts in that respect with liberalism or communitarianism, even the communitarian approach that came to be associated with the Franco-Prussian version of the tradition.

2. Other people or groups will dominate a person to the extent that they are in a position to exercise arbitrary interference in the life of that person, that is, interference that is not subject to the ultimate control of the interferee.

3. Just by virtue of occupying such a position, others will exercise an alien control in the person's life. This control may be mediated via active interference but it may also be mediated by invigilation or intimidation.

4. The value of freedom as nondomination is recognized in the long republican tradition from Cicero down to the period of the American and French Revolutions. It is taken in that tradition to argue for having a state that protects against the private domination of citizens—citizens were generally restricted to propertied males—and that does not itself perpetrate public domination.

5. The ideal of freedom as nondomination was betrayed, ironically, by reformers like Jeremy Bentham and William Paley. They assumed in the age of enlightenment that the state should extend its concern to the freedom of women and workers. But by introducing the ideal of freedom as noninterference they made this extension of concern into something much less demanding than it might have been; it became consistent with the inferior legal status that women and workers endured in the eighteenth century.

6. Nineteenth-century movements that emphasized the wage slavery of industrial workers and the white slavery of women drew, mainly unconsciously, on the republican conception of freedom. They argued that the very subjection or domination of women and workers made them unfree, even when it was not expressed in active interference.

7. There are two great points of contrast between the rival conceptions of freedom. The republican ideal is socially more radical than the alternative, supporting social-democratic policies, and it is also politically more radical, providing the base for working out the form of a constitutional-democratic order.

8. Freedom as nondomination is socially more radical in indicting the very existence of an arbitrary power of interference. Freedom as noninterference is less radical in faulting only the active exercise of such a power of interference.

9. Freedom as nondomination is politically more radical in allowing that the state, provided its interference is suitably controlled, need not reduce the freedom of citizens in coercive, even redistributive, legislation and taxation. Freedom as noninterference is politically less radical in presenting the state as an agency whose coercive laws and measures, no matter how meritorious in other respects, affect people's freedom in just the same way as the interference of the criminal.

10. The challenge for civic republicans is to translate these broad republican lessons into specific proposals and policies for an inclusive society. The state should interfere with others so as to guard against private domination, and it should organize itself so as to guard against public domination. But precisely how should it do these things?

11. The lessons on guarding against private domination can only be worked out in detail with empirical feedback about the effects of different policies. But it is important to identify the areas where policy is likely to be needed and to have an imaginative sense of the different policies possible. This applies in the international as well as the domestic area.

12. There are more general lessons about how to guard against public domination. It is a natural necessity that people live in society under the coercive control of the collectivity. The government of that collectivity will not be dominating for a given citizen just to the extent that it is controlled by the citizenry as a whole and that citizen has an equal share in the exercise of such control.

13. But how are citizens to control government in this way? Conceptually, what republican democracy requires is that government should be directed by the egalitarian expression of common concerns, that is, concerns that are taken as relevant on all sides, even if they are differently weighted.

14. What sorts of institutions does republican democracy—the rule of common concerns—argue for? The broad outlines of an answer can be worked out by consideration of how voluntary associations are likely to control the way they do business.

15. The example of the condominium suggests that any republican democracy will have to organize itself on the basis of a battery of electoral and nonelectoral constraints. It will have to conduct its life on the pattern of the mixed constitution and the contestatory citizenry that are celebrated in republican tradition. This will give an important role to civic deliberation, empowering the considerations that come to be accepted on all deliberative sides as admissible reasons to invoke in public decision-making.

3

THE THEORY IN PRACTICE?

Spain 2004–8

PHILIP PETTIT

THE OBSERVATIONS I SHALL be making on the government of
Spain in the period from March 2004 to June 2007 are presented
at the invitation of Prime Minister José Luis Rodríguez Zapatero.
Mr. Zapatero aligns himself with the long European tradition of
republican, citizen-centered thought and agreed to reply to a lecture I gave in Madrid in 2004 on how this tradition might be used
in the contemporary shaping of government. In response to my
comment that he would find it hard to live up to republican principles, he issued an invitation that I return and provide a republican
review of his government before the next election. So here I am. I
could do no other.

Let me address a few preliminary issues before getting to the
substance of what I have to say. First, I should make clear that I am
not a personal friend or adviser of Zapatero. I have met with him
on two occasions, one when I gave my initial lecture, and the other
when I interviewed him after his second year in government; both
meetings were reported in the press. My detachment is emphasized
by the fact that I have had to prepare the review on the basis of my
own research, in which I have mainly relied on independent, outside commentators.[1] I come to the task before me, then, only as an
umpire—not as a personal friend or adviser, not even as someone
who has been provided with special channels of information.

The second preliminary remark I should make is that in one
important respect my review has to be quite shallow. My focus

is on how far the government's program has been true to republican principles. But the policies that a government adopts on
the basis of principles are also shaped by practical judgments on
the best means for advancing those principles. They are the
product of two forces, one philosophical, the other practical. In
looking at the government's performance from a philosophical
viewpoint, I shall be looking at how far its policies have reflected
a concern for republican principles. But I shall not be making a
judgment on whether the policies adopted were, from a practical
point of view, the best available means for advancing those principles. It is not yet possible to make that sort of assessment; only
time will tell.

The third preliminary remark I should make may be more controversial; it suggests that, however shallow, my review has to be
wider than the document the prime minister asked me to prepare.
Those who assume the reins of government after a Spanish election, like those elected in any advanced democracy, do not govern
on their own. They rule in combination with the governments of
the Autonomous Communities, with the opposing as well as the
supporting parties in parliament, with the professional bureau-
cracy in the ministries, with the judges and other officers who serve
on the courts and tribunals, with the media and civic movements
that keep a vigilant eye on public affairs—and of course with the
monarch or head of state who represents that inclusive community. The life of a democracy is an interactive affair in which there
are many roles to fill, and many hands have to play a part. This
being so, I shall have to make some comments on other aspects of
government apart from the specific contributions of Zapatero and
his party.

I divide what I have to say into three parts. In the first I lay out
the principles that Zapatero has espoused. In the second I look at
how far his government has followed those principles in guarding
against private power. And in the third I look at how far it has followed them in guarding against the abuse of its own public power.
I sum up my finding in a brief conclusion.

I look here only at the domestic performance of government,
not at what it has done on the international stage. There have been

a number of interesting international initiatives taken by Zapatero's government here: for example, in setting up the Alliance of Civilizations within the United Nations, in developing Spanish and European Union relations with Cuba and Latin America generally, in organizing EU action on the problem of refugees, in trying to deal with the refugee problem in negotiation with African states, in making some progress on issues related to Gibraltar and the Western Sahara, and of course in raising the level of Spain's overseas aid by more than a quarter. In these respects Zapatero's Spain has been an outstanding world citizen. With a certain regret, however, I have decided not to discuss international initiatives here. It is not possible in the time available to look at all aspects of the government's performance.

THE PRINCIPLES

Civicism

The principles that Prime Minister Zapatero has endorsed derive from the oldest of European political traditions. This is the tradition of republicanism, in which the state is represented as a public business—a *res publica*, in the Latin phrase. It is the business of the many, to be conducted in response to the views of the many, not an affair of the few. The tradition was originally built out of Athenian ideas. It assumed an institutional form in republican Rome, it enjoyed a renaissance in the medieval city republics of northern Italy, and it shaped some of the landmark regimes and episodes in European history. These include Poland's republic of the nobles; the Dutch republic; English parliamentary resistance and independence; the revolution in Britain's American colonies; and of course the revolution in France.

Although we usually refer to the tradition as republican, it might be better described as one of empowered citizenship. It is a tradition of "civicism" or "*civismo*" or "*ciudadanismo*," in which the public enterprise of the state, the *res publica*, is required to operate under the public's scrutiny and on the public's terms. The state is to be a *civitas*, in another Latin word: a civic body in which the *cives* or citizens are incorporated as the members of a cooperative enterprise. More vividly, in a phrase from the world of the Italian city-republics, it is to be a *civitas sibi princeps*: a civic body that rules itself. There will be special functionaries within this civic body—including perhaps an hereditary head of state—but however important their role, these authorities will all have to discharge their duties to the people's satisfaction. They will operate, as I said, under the public's scrutiny and on the public's terms. There is no one with independent authority, no one above the law. The public forum is the last court of appeal.

Freedom as Nondomination

Zapatero has identified himself, from early in his leadership of the PSOE, with the principles of this republican or civicist tradition. There are many spokespersons for the tradition, historical and philosophical, including many in Spain itself. But as it happens he took his starting point from an account of those principles that I gave in a book published in English in 1997 (Pettit 1997) and in Spanish in 1999 (Pettit 1999). (See also Skinner 1998; Viroli 2002; Ruiz Ruiz 2006.)

On this account of republican ideas, there is one supreme political value—freedom as nondomination—and one ultimate principle of government: to equalize and maximize the enjoyment of such freedom among the citizenry. The civicist state, the *res publica*, should be designed so that its members or citizens do not have a *dominus* or master in any part of their lives. They should be free in the basic sense of not being subjected to the control of any other person or group or organization. They should be their own men and women, able to live without fear or deference, able to make their own choices without begging the indulgence or mercy of others.

When are you going to enjoy freedom as nondomination in relation to others? When are you going to stand equal to them, as citizen to citizen? Very simply, when the civic resources you command as a citizen would make it too difficult or too costly for them to try to interfere with you. They cannot harm you or obstruct you. They cannot threaten you effectively. They cannot even inhibit you. Or at least they cannot do those things without serious risk to themselves. Perhaps I am willing to take that risk, as when I commit a crime against you. But if I am then I will be exposed to the censure of my community—in the criminal case I may even be pursued and punished—and this censure will vindicate and help to restore your position. It will mark you out as someone whose undominated exercise of choice is protected, inviolable space.

When you command such civic resources of protection and vindication, then you will also command respect. You will be able to walk tall among us, your fellow citizens, aware of your standing, aware that we are aware of your standing, and aware that each of us is aware of that shared awareness. You will be able to look us in the eye. You may not be as rich as some others, or as well connected, or as well known and influential. But as a citizen equal with others—as a member of the civic incorporation—you will have all that is required to secure your position. You will be provisioned against the destitution or ignorance or insecurity that would render you unprotectable. And you will be protected against the greater powers of others, even against the greater power of those in government, by the framework of an effective law and by the spirit of a supportive culture.

Domination is not the only evil in life. There are also pain and hunger and isolation—a bottomless pit of ills. So why does the tradition focus on the relief of domination? Why does it make freedom as nondomination the principal aim of government?

There are two reasons for this. First, nondomination is a good that all sides in politics can recognize as a suitable goal for government to pursue; it amounts to freedom in a sense in which it has been celebrated throughout most of European history. And, second, this universally avowable good has the special feature that if it is secured, then many other goods will be ensured as well. Let citizens be guarded against domination and they will have to be guarded against destitution and ignorance and insecurity, against violence and fraud and manipulation, and against the various forms of abuse that government itself may visit on its people.

The rich requirements of freedom as nondomination mark a contrast with the rival, more traditionally liberal idea of freedom as noninterference. In order to enjoy nondomination you will have to have the resources necessary to put you beyond the control of others, even the insidious control that does not need active interference: say, the quiet control of the culturally privileged or the economically advantaged. And in the one case where interference is permitted—in the case where the government is allowed to interfere by taxation or legislation or punishment—that interference will have to be under the control of you and your fellow citizens; it will have to materialize on terms that you would each accept.

The ideal of nondomination has two implications for how things should be done by the state on the domestic front. First, it must reduce the dominating potential of private power, introducing policies that support and reinforce the status that people have as citizens: their ability to walk tall, looking others in the eye. And second, it must be organized and constrained—it must organize and constrain itself—so that its public power does not constitute a force for domination in the life of the very citizens it is formed to serve. The republic has to be an undominating guardian against dominating power.

I turn now to a brief review of the domestic performance of Prime Minister Zapatero and his government over the past three years. I will look first at the measures he has adopted for guarding citizens against the effects of private power and then at the steps he has taken to guard against public domination by the state itself. As mentioned earlier, I shall not be examining the policies he has championed for guarding against international power.

GUARDING AGAINST PRIVATE POWER

There are a number of fronts on which any government will have to act in order to guard its citizens against the danger of domination from private individuals or from private groupings of individuals. First, the government will have to ensure that the infrastructure of nondomination is in place and prospering; this includes the economic and legal system on which most citizens rely for their livelihood and independence. Second, it will have to provide for the empowerment of those who are vulnerable, building a system of social security and an equitable framework for regulating potentially dominating relationships such as those of the workplace and the family. Third, the government will have to provide individuals in general with protection against those who would resort to crime and corruption, even to terror tactics, in order to get their way. And fourth it may have to take steps to restrain those individuals and groupings that are relatively powerful. I will address the performance of the government under each of those headings.

The Infrastructure of Nondomination

There are five key elements in the infrastructure that is required for a widespread enjoyment of freedom as nondomination: (1) a flourishing economy; (2) a reliable rule of law; (3) an inclusive knowledge system; (4) a sound health system; and (5) a sustainable environment.

THE ECONOMY

The state of the economy is of vital importance for republicans, since economic destitution exposes people to domination by the few. The Spanish economy flourished under the Aznar administration and it has continued to do so in the last three years. The annual growth rate has been continually above 3%. The unemployment rate has continued to decline—in the last three years it fell from about 11.5% to 8.5% or lower—and there has been a large increase in the number of jobs available. Throughout this period the inflation rate, while above the European average, has hovered around 2.5%. These are good indicators and show that the present government has not just maintained the prosperity of the Aznar years but continued on an upward trajectory.

There are weaknesses on the economic front, however, that cannot be ignored. The long-term concerns include the low level of research and development and the comparatively low level of productivity (Chislett 2004–9, no. 1). It was said in 2004 that it would require "a Herculean effort" on the part of government to improve these matters, but at least the government has shown itself willing to address the task (Chislett 2004–9, no. 8). By the government's own reckoning, productivity was increasing at a rate of 1% in 2006, whereas the rate of increase in 2004 had been just 0.3% (Government of Spain 2007, 10).

While the percentage of GDP invested in research and development in 2004 was 1% of GDP—1.8% was spent on lotteries in that year—the Government's *Ingenio* plan is to raise this to 2% by 2010; it claims to have increased its own spending on research and development since 2004 by 125% (Chislett 2004–9, no. 31; on the government's claim see Government of Spain 2007, 12). We can only hope that the 2% level of investment in research and development is achieved. The current account deficit is very high and only innovation and investment in high technology are likely to bring it down in the longer term.

THE RULE OF LAW

Article 24 of the Constitution recognizes a fundamental right to obtain effective protection from the courts in the exercise of one's rights and legitimate interests. This is the bedrock on which a rule of law can flourish, as it generally does in Spain; it means that no one is deprived of legal rights as a result of lacking economic means. But there is one problem that has long jeopardized the operation of the judicial system, and the enjoyment of the rule of law, and that is congestion and delay in the courts. This is due to the lack of investment by successive governments; per head of population Spain in 2000 had just a third as many judges as Germany (Majone 1993, 70; Consejo General 2004; Hooper 2006, 333). The Aznar government began to tackle this problem with laws in 2000 and 2002, and the Zapatero government has continued the financial and organizational improvements then begun. According to the government, there have been nearly 800 new judges and prosecutors appointed in Spain since April 2004, and a new Judicial Office has been created with a view to streamlining and fast-tracking the operation of the courts (Government of Spain 2007, 19). Let us hope that these steps are effective.

THE KNOWLEDGE SYSTEM

It is essential for the widespread enjoyment of nondomination that citizens understand and are informed about their society and polity, having the know-how required for a full, engaged life. Such know-how depends ultimately on how well the educational system performs, and here Spain's record is not good. The Organization for Economic Cooperation and Development (OECD) reports paint a bleak picture. In 2003, for example, 30% of students dropped out of secondary education, against an OECD average of 12%; and Spain's public spending on education was twenty-eighth out of thirty countries (OECD 2004). The government has introduced new laws governing education and the universities, and reports that spending on education has increased by 63% since 2004 (Government of Spain 2007, 12). We can only hope that these steps will help improve the situation. One important step that the Government has taken is to introduce education for citizenship, in which children and teenagers will be introduced to the issues of government in a pluralist society, to the different viewpoints on those issues, and to the means whereby they can be resolved in democratic dialogue without secularist belligerence or religious righteousness.[2] (For independent support of the idea see Dworkin 2006.)

THE HEALTH SYSTEM

The enjoyment of freedom as nondomination does not only require a suitable economic, legal, and educational infrastructure. It also depends on the availability of a decent system of public health and medical care, and on the management of the environment in a sustainable manner. The health system in Spain has not been at the focus of government policy over the past three years, except in relation to those suffering incapacities; these have been helped under the Law of Dependency, which I discuss later. The records indicate that, while there is variation between regions, the provisions for health are basically very sound. Spanish longevity figures are exceptionally high and, as one commentator puts it, this "bears testimony to the greatly improved public health system and the healthier Spanish eating habits" (Chislett 2004–9, no. 24). Like other governments in Europe, the government introduced a law to restrict tobacco usage, and it claims that in the first year this reduced the number of smokers by 750,000 (Government of Spain 2007, 15).

THE ENVIRONMENT

Spain faces problems of climate change, with a severe drought over recent years, as well as problems of energy dependency. It remains to be seen how effectively governments can act on such problems, shared as those problems are in many parts of the world. But this government does appear to have been taking suitable steps. Its environmental policy puts it on track to meet the Kyoto protocol requirements and it has invested heavily in desalination plants in order to deal with water shortage (Government of Spain 2007, 19; the Institute of Public Policy Research was not confident that Spain would meet the Kyoto standards, however; see Chislett 2004–9, no. 20). Since the government signed on to the Aarhus convention, moreover, Spanish citizens now have considerable rights in challenging environmental developments to ensure that they meet suitable standards (Sanchis-Moreno 2007). On the energy front the country has become a world leader in the development of wind power (last year this accounted for 9% of Spain's power consumption) and the government is actively committed to developing the use of this technology and championing it in Europe (Chislett 2004–9, no. 33).

Empowering the Disadvantaged

Under the civicist image of government, it is never going to be enough just to provide the infrastructure of nondomination and the means of protecting individuals, for in all societies there will be some individuals in positions of relative powerlessness. Unless these are empowered in relation to the powerful there will be a great deal of domination, however invisible or silent, in the society. Advantages have traditionally accrued to men over women, to those in the mainstream over those outside, to the able-bodied or able-minded over the disabled, to employers over employees, and so on. Unless government does something to rectify such inequalities of advantage and power, the weaker will not be able to stand tall with the stronger, looking them in the eye as citizen to citizen. The prime minister is well keyed to this old republican "eye test." Defending the claim for equal rights on the part of gays and lesbians, he held out a challenge to opponents: "look into the eyes of homosexuals, and tell them they are second-class citizens" (Chislett 2004–9, no. 13).

There are serious questions as to the depth of the government's initiatives on the empowerment front, since Spain still lags behind the larger European countries on crucial welfare indices and since labor relations are still in a state of flux. These questions will continue to be pressed by representatives of the disadvantaged, and I would hope that they will prompt further responses if this government is reelected. But whatever the doubts about the depth of the government's initiatives, there can be no doubts about their breadth and sweep. Since the measures taken are well known, I need do little more than recall some of the main changes initiated by this government.

The Law against Gender Violence (January 2005) protects women against domestic aggression. The Law of Homosexual Marriage (July 2005) enables people of the same sex to form marriages on the same terms as heterosexual couples. The Law of Dependency (January 2007) gives assistance to the disabled and to those who have to stay home to take care of the disabled; unusually, it was passed with opposition support. Finally, the Law of Equality (March 2007) seeks to establish conditions under which women are able to play an equal part with men in public life and the workforce. This law obliges the political parties to have at least 40% women on their electoral lists—from the beginning Zapatero's ministry has been comprised of 50% women—and it requires companies employing more than 250 people to introduce equality plans aimed at eliminating discrimination against women in pay, promotion, and benefits (Chislett 2004–9, no. 33).

Apart from these laws, the government has also taken other steps to empower the less powerful. One important departure was the 2005 amnesty for illegal workers. Nearly 700,000 illegal workers, mainly from Latin America and Eastern Europe, were granted an amnesty, if they had an employment contract and had lived in Spain for six months or more (Chislett 2004–9, nos. 11 and 22). This helped guard these people against exploitation but it also increased tax and social security revenues. There is a danger that frequent resort to amnesty measures of this kind might attract further illegal immigration. Future regularization should depend on using the stricter mechanism, described as *arraigo*, which requires illegal immigrants to meet a three-year residency requirement and hold an employment contract of more than one year (Chislett 2004–9, no. 31).

One of the continuing problems in Spain has been the proportion of workers, roughly a third, on short-term contracts. These contracts not only cause insecurity but also have other disadvantages, such as making it difficult to obtain a mortgage. In 2006 the government agreed to a package of reforms with employers and trade unions in an attempt to rectify this problem. Any employee who has held two or more temporary contracts totaling more than 24 months in a 30-month period obtains the right to a permanent contract. The deal will be sweetened by the fact that companies are to be subsidized over two to three years for every worker transferred to such a contract (Chislett 2004–9, no. 25). This measure, together with the demands in the Law of Equality, may also have been made more palatable for companies by the fact that corporation tax was reduced to 30% from the previous 35% (Chislett 2004–9, no. 21). It remains to be seen whether the reforms prove effective in dealing with the problem of *temporalidad*. The fact that so many are employed in construction and tourism suggests that it may not be a durable fix.

The growth in the Spanish economy has driven housing prices to a level where houses have become hard to purchase for less well-off families and younger people. The government has sought to deal with this problem by setting aside land for protected, public housing, and subsidizing such housing in other ways, as well as by providing incentives for owners to rent property (Government of Spain 2007, 17). The problem these measures are designed to deal with may evaporate, if housing prices fall. Such a fall would cause other serious difficulties, however, as people find they are mortgaged for more than their houses are worth. Household indebtedness is already high in Spain, and this would exacerbate those difficulties further.

Protecting the Citizenry

By all accounts of how the state should act, the protection of citizens against the direct and indirect effects of crime is of prime importance. This is particularly true under a civicist approach, since crime involves the assumption of a position of domination over others. The direct crime of violence or theft or fraud makes victims aware of the control exercised by others in their lives, but such control is equally assumed and exercised by those who commit crimes, say of corruption, where the victims may not be aware of the harm they suffer.

Spain is fortunate in having a crime rate that, despite increases over the last twenty years, is lower than the average across the main European countries (Van Dijk 2005).[3] Robbery is a serious problem, but crimes of violence and homicides are lower than average and have been falling over the past three years (Government of Spain 2007, 14). Apart from the threat of terrorism (more on this in a moment), there are problems on two main fronts, one to do with drug cartels and the other with corruption. The first problem derives from Spain's geographical position, which makes it ideal for trafficking in drugs, and so for the operations of organized crime. In its more serious form, the other problem comes from the great boom in the housing sector, which has created enormous opportunities for corruption in the zoning of land for development and in real-estate dealings. Invited to prepare a report on this sector by the government, a United Nations special advisor, Miloon Kothari, described the culture that he found in

2006 as one of "unbridled speculation" and "extreme" corruption (Chislett 2004–9, no. 7).

Is the government doing enough to tackle these problems? On the housing front, it is currently negotiating a law of the land, designed to curb speculation and to make the release of land for development more transparent (Government of Spain 2007, 17). In December 2006 it introduced a law for the prevention of fiscal fraud that ought to reinforce these measures, as should the new Center for Intelligence against Organized Crime. Police operations in Marbella in 2005 revealed the presence of organized crime in the housing sector, and in 2006 the government dissolved the town government after the mayor and three town councilors were imprisoned on charges of corruption and profiteering (Chislett 2004–9, no. 23). These are positive signs, though they fall short of an assurance that the problems will be effectively resolved.

Terrorism is a special problem in Spain. The evil and tragedy that terrorism represents was highlighted in the events of March 11, 2004, when Madrid suffered the effects of an international form of terrorism. But terror has long been a feature of democratic Spain, as a result of the ETA campaign for Basque independence. The latest ETA bombing in Madrid airport in January 2007 occurred even while the government was involved in negotiations with that body. I do not have any base on which to assess the measures taken for protecting the citizenry against these terrorist threats, national and international, though I should add that to an outside eye the response of the police, the courts, and the government to the March 11 tragedy has been firm and unhysterical—a model for the world.

Was it proper for the government to have held talks with ETA, as it did, without that body having renounced the use of force? The history of many countries, including my native Ireland, suggests that the path to peace may often require talks with violent groups. And such talks are needed prior to the renunciation of force, if only to establish the terms on which force will be renounced. This truth may be unsavory but it is the merest common sense. Did the government make a radical departure from established practice in opening talks with ETA? The opposition has fiercely condemned the government for its efforts, citing the 2000 antiterrorist pact between the parties. But academic commentators suggest that this condemnation rings hollow, given the record of the Aznar government in trying to deal on the same terms with ETA. As one academic commentator puts it, "The Partido Popular disagreement with the Socialists" is based, not on a real difference between past and present responses to ETA, but "on a fanciful interpretation of Zapatero's radical departure from traditional policy" (Celso 2006, 132).

Although the levels of crime are good compared with those in Europe as a whole, Spain has a very high prison population. In June 2006 it had 146 prisoners per 100,000 population, the highest figure in the European Union, and this has led to severe overcrowding in the prisons (Chislett 2004–9, no. 26). A society should be judged by how well it treats those who offend, as well as those who are offended against, and I worry about the conditions of those held under current conditions. I also have a concern about the way ETA prisoners are distributed to prisons all over Spain, not held in prisons in or near the Basque country. However appalling the deeds of ETA, this pattern looks like a needless and arbitrary imposition that must cause immense hardship for the families of these offenders. The state must behave to the highest standards, especially when it has recourse to the instruments of criminal punishment, and I would like to see a future Spanish government take on these problems.

Restraining the Strong

In an advanced democracy like Spain, those who are relatively more powerful do most damage to people's freedom as nondomination insofar as they exercise undue influence over government. By undue influence I mean influence that is not defensible on public grounds that would be widely invoked and accepted across the society. In this respect it is distinct from the influence of nongovernmental organizations that make their arguments in public and frame them in publicly accepted terms. It is the sort of influence to which parties and politicians quietly succumb, not for avowable reasons of national interest, but for reasons of personal or party advantage.

There are many potential sources and many potential forms of undue influence, and one measure of a healthy democracy is the extent to which it maintains a constant watch against the danger. In most democracies the most powerful influence comes via campaign finance and the associated lobbying of government. In Spain the effect of this influence is tempered by campaign finance restrictions and the party discipline that a parliamentary system imposes. The governing party or parties have to stick together in a parliamentary system in order to maintain the administration, by contrast with the situation in the Washington system, so individual legislators or ministers cannot be lobbied individually to any great effect. A lobby group has to persuade a whole party, or at least a whole cabinet, in order to get its way on any serious issue. This makes for a happy contrast with the situation in the United States, or indeed in many Latin American countries.

This aspect of the Spanish system means that, short of corruption gaining a hold, the undue influence of corporations is limited. The most salient sign of undue but still legal influence may be in the lowering of the corporate tax rate, which was prompted by the existence of lower rates elsewhere in Europe. There is a danger of European countries racing one another to the bottom in a desire to attract corporate investment, and the obvious solution has to be a Europe-wide agreement not to let this happen. I would hope that the government of Spain will work toward that end in future years.

But if there is a reasonable separation between business and state in Spain, there is still no proper separation between church and state. The agreement with the Catholic Church in 1979 was that it would become self-financing after six years, with the help of a provision whereby members of the church could opt, as in Germany, for a small percentage of their taxes to be paid to the church. Despite the taxation arrangement, the church did not assume its self-financing responsibility at the agreed time and has continued to obtain massive state subsidies; these have been provided, presumably, for fear that the church would mobilize opposition to any party that did not continue to provide financial support. The abuse was somewhat balanced as government began to make funds available to other faiths too (see Hooper 2006, 98–99 on these issues). But abuse it surely remains. Why should the citizens of a country as a whole be required to provide funding for the upkeep of any religious bodies, however admirable those bodies may be?

The Zapatero government has at last reached a more reasonable accommodation with the church. It will be possible for taxpayers to earmark a higher percentage of their taxes for the church (0.7% rather than 0.52%) but the government will no longer provide an annual contribution to make up the difference between the church's income and expenditure. The church will also have to provide a report on how it spends the money received from taxpayers (Chislett 2004–9, no. 28). These are sensible arrangements and long overdue. The government has also reached an accommodation with the church over the teaching of religion in schools. This is a matter of detailed compromise, however, and it is hard to adjudicate from an outside perspective.

Guarding against Public Power

Background

We now have a picture of the policies that the Zapatero government has pursued and the extent to which they can be seen as civicist policies, designed to guard people's freedom as nondomination against private power. But how has the government done on the other domestic front on which I promised to assess it? How well or how far has it worked to guard citizens against the danger from its own public power? The government has made a point of complying faithfully with existing constraints of transparency, accountability, and responsiveness. These are designed to make an elected government nondominating, even as it forms and enacts the policies governing people's lives. But has it done anything to improve the organization whereby government action is meant to assume a nondominating profile?

The traditional mode of protecting against public domination was already well worked out in classical republican sources. It consists in subjecting those in government to a battery of constraints, most of them associated with what Roman and Renaissance republicans hailed as the mixed constitution. Under this sort of constitution there were to be a large number of public offices and bodies—some involved the people acting as a whole, some empowered elected officials, some gave power even to inherited authorities. These officials and bodies were to constrain one another so that any legislation or policy that passed challenges on all sides would be more or less bound to reflect what was thought of as the common good. The idea was that, if a measure proved defensible to various sectors in the society, it would not constitute the exercise of an uncontrolled power of domination in their lives.

By republican lights, then, everyone would be able to view the state as a necessary but undominating source of restriction and coordination. They would not see the hand of an unchecked, arbitrary master in the doings of government. They would see in those doings a hand that was forced to treat them as worthy of equal respect with others.

Three Positive Steps

The government has not sought any constitutional amendment over the last three years. This is not surprising since the Spanish democratic constitution and tradition does well in ensuring fulfillment of the conditions that are required for republican or civic legitimacy. That shows up in the fact that it is placed sixteenth in the Economist Intelligence Unit's index of democracy among 167 countries, ahead of the United States, the United Kingdom, and France (Kekic 2007).[4] It scores very high on the two components in that index that are especially relevant to our purposes: the quality of the electoral process and the protection of civil liberties.[5]

While not seeking any constitutional amendment over the last three years, however, the government did take other steps to reduce the possibility of domination by those in authority and power. They include the move to give parliament more power in overseeing government; the introduction of greater discipline in the presentation of government data; and the independence given to the national television station.

A number of minor adjustments have strengthened the position of the parliament in relation to government. One is the introduction of the law whereby parliament is required to approve the sending of Spanish troops on active duty abroad (Chislett 2004–9, no. 18). Related developments are the initiatives whereby the prime minister holds a monthly question period in the senate, and has renounced the right to favor questions from his own party either in the senate or in the congress (Government of Spain 2007, 24). In a parliamentary democracy like Spain the government can usually be assured of controlling the legislative vote but recourse to parliament is important on a number of counts. It makes for transparency in government, since parliament is conducted in public. It allows for the interrogation of policy and the formation of objections and questions. And of course it makes it possible, in principle, for the government to be defeated.

There are also some minor changes in the presentation of government data that are worth recording and applauding. The law of institutional publicity whereby government funds cannot be spent on party propaganda, only on matters of clear public interest and utility, is an excellent initiative (Government of Spain 2007, 24). So are the announced changes whereby data and statistics are to be made increasingly available on the internet, including data and statistics on the quarterly public accounts and on the economic presuppositions of government policy-making. These measures should help to guard against the problem that existing channels of information can be slow or biased, though they do not address the equally important problem, present in almost all democracies, that such information is often incomplete; government agencies are often unwilling to release information on their doings. Transparency legislation needs to be supported by legislation on freedom of information.

Perhaps the most significant change that Zapatero has introduced to guard against domination by government is the transformation whereby RTVE, the national television broadcaster, has been made independent and autonomous—and, by all accounts, has already begun to prove itself so (Chislett 2004–9, no. 15). The board is appointed by parliament on the basis of a two-thirds majority and it then selects its director general. This is a splendid innovation for both substantive and symbolic reasons. Substantively, it makes it possible to have a credible commentator and critic of government that is not tied up with any private corporation and that has an incentive to prove itself autonomous. And symbolically, it testifies to the fact that civic or republican democracy does not mean dictatorship by the party in power; the public retains maximum resources for keeping tabs on government and for calling government to account. I had the policy of independence for the public broadcaster in mind when I told Prime Minister Zapatero in 2004 that he would find it hard stay faithful to his proclaimed objectives. I am very happy to record that I was wrong. On this matter, he has kept the civicist faith. Or at least he will have done so, if public funding for the national broadcaster is maintained at an appropriate level.

Greater Regional Autonomy

There is a further set of changes I should mention in connection with the organization of government: the new statutes that the government has backed for Catalonia and other Autonomous Communities. These changes have been important for the extent to which they accommodate regional aspirations that cannot be silenced or repressed in a free democracy and also for the way in which they promote the dispersion and decentralization of power. As regional and national voices have a shared input on local developments in health, education, policing, and even financial matters, those developments ought to have a greater chance of being shaped by the terms on which citizens should expect them to be decided. To that extent, there ought to be a smaller chance of decisions being made for sectional advantage: say, for the advantage of a particular party or region, profession, union, or corporation. There ought to be a better prospect for nonarbitrary and nondominating government.

Let me stop for a moment to emphasize this point. If a community is governed in some areas from two centers of power, with different forums of accountability, then the chance increases that no one will be dominated by government decisions; special factional or sectional interests will balance and help to check one another. We see this in the way that European Union institutions have reinforced bodies like the Spanish Audit Court, and offices like that of the *defensor del pueblo* (ombudsman) in fighting against corruption (see (Magone 2004, 73). The empowerment of the Autonomous Communities within a framework where central government inevitably retains its own role can serve as an important way of keeping government honest and fair. The principle that applies here is the old republican principle according to which powers should be separated into many hands; this is the principle that argues also for the independence of the judiciary from government.

There is another side, of course, to the issue of regional autonomy, and I cannot just ignore it here. The Spanish system of Autonomous Communities has a rainbow character, with some communities enjoying more autonomy than others; this is the product of historical diversity, which is given formal recognition in the law and constitution. Because of this rainbow character, however, any change in the statute of a single community is liable to generate some instability. It is liable to prompt other communities to play catch-up and try to restore the previous balance. This raises a question. Was it unduly dangerous for the government to allow the change in Catalonia? Did it risk balkanization, for example, as the opposition alleged?

Spanish democracy cannot hold together unless all parts can think of themselves as incorporating voluntarily in "a project," to quote from Ortega y Gasset, for "a life in common" (Ortega y Gasset 2003, 121). Thus the terms of incorporation are bound to be subject to periodic review and amendment, and adjustments such as those introduced in Catalonia and other communities are only to be expected. The stability of Spain has to be dynamic in nature, not static; it has to emerge from an ongoing, mutually respectful project of building a life in common. The point is presumably recognized on both sides of politics, since some adjustments have been supported by the opposition party as well as by the government.

But is a continuing process of adjustment likely to lead to the balkanization or breakup of Spain? The historical linkages of the communities, and the benefits derived from the project of incorporation in a single country—particularly in view of Spain's membership in the European Union—should make the prospect of breakup extremely unlikely. Those linkages and benefits are firm and salient enough to ensure mainstream, democratic support for Spanish affiliation in the most independent of the communities, as opinion polls continue to show. The only danger is that the fear of balkanization, and the associated distrust of the communities, may nurture an aggressive centralism and elicit a countervailing movement for independence. The Partido Popular comes close to embracing such an aggressive centralism. Thus it has challenged the constitutional status of the Catalonian statute before the Tribunal Constitucional and, by some accounts, has sought to exert political influence over members of the court (Chislett 2004–9, no. 32). Does anyone think that the way to preserve Spanish unity is to resort to the courts in the hope of overthrowing a measure that has been approved by the Catalan and Spanish parliaments and supported by nearly 75% in a Catalan referendum? That confrontational path could prove to be the high road to the very balkanization it is supposed to avoid.

Opposition, Courts, and Civic Movements

Before concluding this overview, I should mention three respects in which the organization of the Spanish polity, by my lights, has been failing in recent times. They do not directly involve the government but, as I said at the beginning, government is not just the business of the party in power—not, at least, in a proper civic democracy. My critical remarks relate to the opposition, to the courts, and to the civic movements that operate in the society.

The role of the opposition—"the loyal opposition"—in a parliamentary democracy is to force government to justify its policies in open parliament, raise hard questions about those policies, and campaign for what it sees as superior alternatives. What it must not do is to try to render the country ungovernable; that would be a betrayal of the system to which it owes loyalty. Yet to my outside eye, and to other commentators, that is precisely what the opposition appears to be attempting. Thus one very measured and respected commentator, William Chislett, has written in different reports of "the policy of maximum hostility" adopted by the opposition, its "zero cooperation," its "hysterical standpoint," and "its permanent state of confrontation with the government" (see Chislett 2004–9, nos. 20, 21, and 23). And Jesús de Polanco, chairman of PRISA, the owner of *El País*, has suggested that the opposition "believes that anything goes in order to recover power" (Chislett 2004–9, no. 33). The civicist picture is that all sides need to be given a respectful hearing in politics, and the government's emphasis on dialogue reflects this, as did its policy of "tranquil opposition" when out of office. The current opposition rejects that picture, it appears, in favor of a fundamentalist, polarizing image. In their projection, the government is a demonic force that they, the only good and rightful representatives of Spain, are required to fight by any means, fair or foul. This image ill serves democracy—or common sense.

The role of the judiciary in a parliamentary democracy is to stand apart from politics and be ready to make judgments on the legal merits of every case, in indifference to the positions taken by political parties. In order to ensure this the Consejo General del Poder Judicial was set up as a body for appointing judges to all courts other than the Tribunal Constitucional. My impression is that this judicial independence has been compromised, at least in the general perception. The assumption that appointees to the Consejo General del Poder Judicial will defend a partisan point of view appears to be widely endorsed, in flagrant distortion of the founding idea behind that body. This may be due to the shift to a parliamentary system of appointment, which was made by the socialist government in 1985; it encourages party attempts to game the system, as in the reluctance of the current opposition to agree to a new set of appointments (Hooper 2006, 336). The Consejo is now accepted as, in the words of one writer, "sometimes a heavily politicized body" (Magone 2004, 72). Even worse, there now appears to be a growing belief that the Tribunal Constitucional, for long an institution greatly admired for its independence (Magone 2004, 72), has begun to succumb to political pressures (Chislett 2004–9, no. 32). The very existence of these perceptions and beliefs suggests that major steps need to be taken in order to reinforce the independence of the judiciary from party politics. This may even be an area where constitutional reform is required.

A third feature about the organization of the Spanish polity relates to the way that the civic invigilation of government is exercised. In a complex society, the exercise of civic vigilance cannot be conducted by individuals alone, since the informational demands are too heavy. It is best conducted via independent, nongovernmental organizations. These will have to be supported from a mix of public and private sources but they must be independent from government and command respect in the population at large. Only bodies of such a kind can monitor government with a professional level of expertise for its performance in relation to a variety of causes: for example, women's issues, environmental concerns, consumer rights, health issues, and prisoners' rights. The interest in civic vigilance over government is evident in Spain from the number of mass demonstrations. But the proper conduct of civic invigilation requires the expertise of nongovernmental organizations, and I worry that these do not have a sufficiently strong presence in Spanish civil life . While nongovernmental organizations apparently command widespread esteem, only one in four Spaniards actually belongs to a civil organization—a low figure by European standards (Magone 2004, 34–37; Fishman 2007).

CONCLUSION

It may be useful, in conclusion, if I summarize the general drift of my findings and impressions. I have tried to look at the domestic initiatives of the Zapatero government from a republican or civicist point of view in which the aim of government is to reduce private domination without perpetrating public domination.

I looked first at the policies for guarding against private and then at those for guarding against public domination.

Private domination is facilitated by general inefficiencies such as those of an unbalanced if buoyant economy, a cumbersome judicial system, and a below-average educational sector. It is generated by certain more specific problems. These include personal vulnerability, whether sponsored by physical, economic, or cultural disadvantage; communal exposure to crime and terrorism; and the undue power of corporate bodies, commercial or ecclesiastical.

The government has not been able to eliminate the general inefficiencies listed but has put policies in place, often building on those of the Aznar government, that should help in time to reduce them. It has taken courageous, cutting-edge initiatives in dealing with the vulnerabilities of women, homosexuals, illegal migrants, the incapacitated, and workers on temporary contracts. It has faced the terrorist threat squarely, although ETA dealt a serious blow to its sensible attempts to negotiate a settlement. And, finally, it has rectified in good part the historical anomaly of continuing state subsidies to the Roman Catholic Church.

The dangers of public domination are as familiar as those of private. Domination will be more likely to the extent that a government is secretive about information, for example, hostile to parliamentary debate, impatient about an independent media, and anxious to concentrate power in its own hands. When a government leans in these directions, it becomes a power in people's lives that they cannot effectively monitor or check.

The Zapatero government has been less secretive, less hostile to parliament, less impatient of an independent media, and less anxious to keep power to itself than comparable administrations. Indeed it has taken some bold steps. It has established a law of publicity, given more attention and power to parliament, made the national broadcaster statutorily independent, and supported greater autonomy in the communities.

I do not say that on these two fronts the government has scored ten out of ten. There are further steps that I suggested it should take in a number of areas. If it is reelected, I hope that it will strengthen the welfare rights of the disadvantaged, deal with the severe overcrowding in prisons, deepen the transparency of government by entrenching the concept of freedom of information, and take whatever measures are possible for restoring confidence in an independent judiciary.

But if the steps taken by the government leave some room for improvement, the striking thing is that it has taken so many steps in the right direction. I do not know how this government will fare in the turmoil of electoral politics, nor when the Tribunal Constitucional passes judgment on the Catalan Statute. But I do know this. The Zapatero administration has kept faith with the civicist or republican vision of government. And in doing so, it has set exemplary standards of honesty, courage, and effectiveness. Despite the enormous challenges confronted in the last few years, it has maintained a steady direction and made Spain into a model for how an advanced democracy can perform.

Appendix

CHALLENGES AND QUERIES

I WAS GENERALLY PLEASED with the responses to my lecture both in public presentations and in press interviews and commentary. But naturally there were critical as well as supportive responses, and I take this opportunity to reply to a number of the issues raised. Many of these were first aired in the open letter that Pedro J. Ramírez, editor of *El Mundo*, addressed to me in his newspaper on June 3, 2007 (Ramírez 2007). This letter covered a great deal of ground and was written on the basis of a text of the lecture that had been leaked to *El Mundo* over a week before the formal presentation.

In allowing greater autonomy for the Autonomous Communities, and in seeking to satisfy nationalistic aspirations among the Catalan people, the Zapatero government has put the very unity and existence of Spain at risk. There is now a real prospect, in a phrase that the opposition frequently uses, that Spain will be balkanized: that it will break up in the way that Yugoslavia broke up. This is supported by the fact that some nationalists in the Autonomous Communities have begun to speak of a Montenegro resolution for their grievances.

I have found that there is a good deal of concern in Spain about balkanization and that it explains the degree of hostility that some people seem to feel for the Catalan Statute. But my own view from outside of Spain is that this concern is born of fantasy and has no place in serious politics. There is absolutely no danger of the country breaking up or going through anything that might deserve to be described as a process of balkanization.

Those who worry about balkanization think of the unity of Spain as being based on the anticentrifugal pull exerted from the Madrid center that holds the parts in place. The image is gravitational. As the planets stay in place, and do not veer away on centrifugal paths of their own, because of the gravitational pull of the sun, so it is said to be with at least some Autonomous Communities. Their natural disposition is to go their own centrifugal way and it is only the pull from the center that keeps them attached to the whole. Those who think in terms of this image are naturally worried about any relaxation in the hold that Madrid exerts over the communities and any readiness to grant greater autonomy.

But it is not just the anticentrifugal force exerted from Madrid that holds Spain together. Now that Spain and its regions are so embedded, and embedded with such benefit, in the European Union, this unifying force has been supplemented by an even more powerful centripetal force that is exerted from Brussels. This force adds a push from the outside that complements the pull from within and thereby ensures the continued unity of Spain as a national and international entity.

The push from outside is not hard to understand. The member countries of the European Union each have a veto over the admission of any new member, including a newly independent unit that secedes from an existing member. Would any member country be inclined to veto the admission of a breakaway region from an existing member country? Well, that original member country would certainly be disposed to exercise a veto. And, equally certainly, it would be joined by others in doing so. A great many member countries have regions that would happily break away if it were feasible for them to do so and allowing any region to leave an existing member and rejoin the Union in its own right would massively boost the feasibility of such secession. Thus it is as certain as these things get to be that no region in an existing member country can expect to be admitted as a member in its own right, if it breaks away from that country, or at least if it breaks away without agreement on both sides.

The diverse communities of Spain are held together by the European centripetal force as well as by the Spanish anticentrifugal force and, once this is put in the picture, it seems silly to raise a concern about balkanization. That might have been a reasonable concern prior to Spain's entry to the European Union but it is a concern that should now be put aside and banished from serious discussion. No Autonomous Community that values membership in the European Union can seriously aspire to independence. And no central government that recognizes this should seriously worry about such aspirations. If the specter of balkanization continues to be raised, that is only because it makes for good, scaremongering politics, not because it serves the cause of good government.

But you should realize that some Autonomous Communities are now exercising the right to control education and culture in a way that undermines the unity of Spain. There are even Spanish parents in Catalonia, for example, who would wish to have their children educated through Spanish and cannot do so.

The concern raised here is not one of balkanization but one of dehispanization, as we might call it. The specter is not that Spain may go the way of Yugoslavia but that it may go the way of Switzerland. The threat is swissification, not balkanization.

Should all children in Spain be educated primarily through the Spanish language? It might make for greater fluidity in the conduct of public and indeed private business were this the case and that may be an important pragmatic consideration. But I see no reason in principle why that consideration should triumph over the wish of a region of the country to impose a language other than Spanish in its schools. Switzerland operates perfectly well, despite the fact that its various regions differ in the languages they employ. And in Spain, unlike Switzerland, there will always be one language, Spanish, that is available to all, whether as a first or second language.

But people in Switzerland who speak one language have always known that, if they move to another region, they may have to see their children educated through a different language. This has not been the case in Spain until recent years, it may be said, so that parental expectations as to how their children would be educated have often been disappointed.

The use of Catalan in schools is not so very recent that many parents can have been surprised by the practice in that community; it goes back well before Zapatero's government. But there may be a case for a transitional arrangement, perhaps over another decade or so, whereby the central government would provide support for such parents and their children. For example, the central government might provide subsidies for relevant families to have their children educated in private, Spanish-speaking schools.

What of families who see their history or future in Catalonia, to continue to take it as an example, but who speak Spanish at home and wish to have their children educated through that language? Should there be some accommodation made for them, even after a transitional arrangement has ceased? I do not think that there is a requirement in justice to make such an accommodation. It is just a hard fact of life that people can only expect to have their children given a public education in the language of the relevant public. The truth is that once Catalonia was given control over its own educational system, the relevant public became the Catalan public.

You comment on the rainbow character of the Spanish state: the fact that its different communities have different degrees of autonomy in relation to the center. Doesn't this mean that any change in the statute of one community is likely to trigger a round of changes, leading to an unstable situation in which everything is in constant flux?

Spain is certainly unusual in having a constitution under which there are a number of constituent communities that relate to the center in ways that allow different degrees of autonomy. Those different degrees of autonomy reflect historical variations in the extent to which the communities regard themselves as identified with the Spanish polity as a whole. Hence it is unlikely that communities like Catalonia and the Basque country would be happy to have all communities enjoy the same degree of autonomy, no matter how high. These communities have an investment in having a greater degree of autonomy—or at least sharper markers of identity—that emphasize their distinctive character and relationship to the whole.

The rainbow character of the Spanish polity—this community of communities—does mean that any change in the statute of one is likely to set off a round of changes involving others, and a round of constitutional challenges to the right of various communities to make the changes introduced. Indeed, we have seen evidence of that cycle over the past few years. But is that factor enough on its own to argue for freezing relationships at their current level? I do not think so.

No multicommunal state like Spain can expect to advance and develop, as it is currently doing, without shifts in the expectations and demands of its people and, in particular, of its different communities of people. It would be a recipe for antagonism and resentment to lay it down as a principle that these shifting attitudes could never give rise to adjustments in the constitutional order or in the statutes whereby different communities relate to the center. Hence I think that there is no option but to accept that there will be adjustments of this kind over the years and that there is no steady state, no equilibrium, at which things will finally settle.

That is why I said that the stability for which Spain must look is a dynamic stability in which it is recognized that different parts of the whole will occasionally seek structural changes and in which there is a readiness to debate about the changes sought without any fear or panic about balkanization. A shared recognition that there is no danger of balkanization should provide a firm basis for unhurried, unpanicked consideration of the changes that may be called for at any time. There is no reason to expect that changes will be continually demanded in a time-consuming cycle of constitutional debate. The forces of electoral politics should ensure that this does not happen, since people's patience would surely wear thin if politicians were to pursue endless change.

I should also say that I think Spain may be better off as a result of having an arrangement under which it is accepted that there will be various adjustments and accommodations over time. An absolutely fixed, amendment-proof order may seem to promise quiet and peace, but the sort of quiet and peace it provides can be very bad for democracy. It can lead to a culture in which change is sought by legal subterfuge and backdoor recourse to the courts rather than in forthright political demand and debate. Such a culture would benefit elites at a cost to the public.

Don't you take too soft a line on ETA and on terrorism more generally in suggesting that it is appropriate for the government to have talks with such a group before it lays down arms?

I do not think that a government should negotiate with a terrorist group unless there are signs that it is at least willing to call a ceasefire; that would almost certainly be counterproductive. But the government had talks with ETA at a time when there was a ceasefire in place, though there was not a formal renunciation of violence. I stand strongly by my claim that it would be irresponsible of government not to be willing to deal with a terrorist organization under such conditions. It may be satisfying to adopt a moralistic stance and declare that you will never talk with men and women of violence. But such moral purism is out of place when a cause as important as that of communal peace is at stake. This is recognized worldwide and as a matter of age-old wisdom. Government sometimes has to sup with the devil in order to protect its citizens from what the devil may visit upon them.

Things might be different in a situation where a terrorist movement could be broken up by force and without too much collateral bloodshed or damage. But that situation is extremely rare. In most contexts it will not be possible to defeat an ongoing terrorist movement by force of arms or not at least without a high and unacceptable level of violence. And where the movement has some support in the community, the attempt to defeat it by force of arms, in disregard for the possibility of dialogue, will often serve to recruit more members to its ranks. Not only was it right for the Zapatero government to hold talks with ETA, I believe that the display of willingness to enter into dialogue may prove to have been beneficial in the long term. It may prove to have made it more difficult for ETA to recruit more members into active service.

But apart from the talks issue, you argue that the government ought to reconsider its policy of holding ETA prisoners in prisons that are far way from the Basque country and so from their families. And to many in Spain that will certainly seem to be much too soft a line to take.

I do not say that ETA members should be given special privileges in how the criminal justice system deals with them. I only say that they should not be subject to special disadvantages, at least not on an arbitrary basis. If there is a rationale for the present policy of dispersing ETA prisoners throughout Spain, then the government ought to publicize and defend this justification.

It is not common practice in any civilized justice system to imprison offenders at such a distance from their home that it is impossible or difficult for family to keep in touch. Nor is it sensible practice. There is evidence that the closer the contact that prisoners maintain with their families, the better the chance of their rehabilitation. The practice of housing ETA prisoners away from the Basque country is, on the face of it, a way of imposing an extra punishment over and beyond that which the courts may have licensed. The government may have a security rationale for its practice but, if so, this should be publicly explained in justification of the policy.

When the state confines convicted offenders in prison, it is duty-bound to see that this is done in a manner that is civilized and, I would say, respectful of the rights of prisoners. Prisons are meant to restrain offenders and penalize them but the restraint imposed should not go beyond that which is strictly required by the considerations of restraint and punishment licensed under the civic culture and the legal regime. We know that prisons worldwide offend against this principle; for example, a recent study in some U.S. states suggests that ten percent of male offenders are raped in prison (Kaiser 2007). I worry about Spanish prisons, not just for the way ETA prisoners are distributed around the country, but also for the overcrowded conditions that apparently prevail there.

Isn't it naive of you to suggest that the way that Spain has dealt with the March 11 bombings has been a model of moderation and a lesson for the world? After all, there has been a consistent claim by the opposition, and by some newspapers, that evidence on an ETA involvement has been suppressed.

I cannot make a personal judgment on the claim about the suppression of evidence. But it has to be said that outside commentators and the vast bulk of Spanish commentators do not seem to take that claim seriously any more. On the basis of these testimonial indicators, I can only regard the charge as unsubstantiated.

In speaking of the moderation of the Spanish response to March 11, I had two facts in mind. The first is that the law and the government have not responded to the outrage by taking steps that would put civil liberties in danger and warp the processes of the courts. This cannot be said for other countries in similar conditions. The second fact is that there is no evidence in Spain of any backlash against Muslim communities in the wake of the 2004 bombings. This speaks to an admirable level of tolerance and understanding, and one that makes Spain quite special among countries that have been exposed to similar atrocities.

You say at one point in your lecture that you think that government in a parliamentary system like Spain's is more resistant to special influences than government under the sort of presidential system in the United States. Do you mean to suggest that there are no problems, then, of business-government collusion in Spain— contrary to some recent allegations?

I do not mean to suggest that there is never this sort of collusion under the Spanish system, though I am absolutely not in a position to make a judgment on any recent allegations. But I do think it is worth stressing that the Spanish system is less vulnerable to problems of special influence than the American.

In the Spanish system, and in parliamentary systems generally, the fact that the administration or government is elected by parliament means that supporters in the legislature have to vote in general for the government or risk causing its collapse. But that in turn has two important effects. It means, first, that the administration can develop a coherent legislative program and see it through parliament more or less confidently; the government can act like a unified agent—a corporate entity. And it means, second, that members of the parliament on the government side have their hands more or less tied on the issue of how to vote; they vote as the party or coalition in government requires them to vote.

Both effects have beneficial results. The first means that government can be responsive to aggregate public opinion; it has the capacity to gauge where opinion is going, or where it can be led by political initiative, and to reflect it in policy-making. The second means that members of parliament are not exposed to pressures from local interests in their constituency, or from lobbying on behalf of special interests more generally; their votes are not available to be pressured or purchased.

These effects are reversed in the American system. The fact that the administration is elected independently means that there is no strict requirement on the parliament or congress to go along with government; hence the regularity with which party members cross the floor. That means, first, that the government cannot confidently plan or promise any coherent program of legislation; a new majority has to be found for every bill, and can often be found only by means of offering individual representatives special favors for their constituencies. And it means, second, that members of the congress are exposed to the full pressure of local and lobbying interests on the matter of how they are to vote. This pressure is particularly intense, since politicians depend on the financial support of such interests for their election campaigns.

The upshot is that government under the Spanish system is capable of much more effective legislation—this is surely evident in the rich program introduced by the Zapatero government—and is much less vulnerable to the influence of business lobbies and the like. Undoubtedly, those forces have an effect. But on matters of substance the influence they wield has to be exerted via a proposal to the party in power, taken as a whole, or to one or another minister. And in either case there will usually have to be an argument put forward for the proposal that is framed in generally acceptable terms. These safeguards are not guarantees against collusion but they certainly guard against the free-for-all chaos of a congress in which there will always be marginal votes that are subject to the control of the most powerful lobby.

These considerations only apply, of course, on matters where the legislature has to rule and many hands are involved. They are not relevant to decisions that are in the gift of an individual official of government or a small-scale body. That is why things are very different in local government, particularly with decisions on matters like the zoning of land for development. Such decisions can be made away from the sunlight of debate and publicity and are particularly susceptible to the influence of special interests, even to the influence that is mediated, in outright corruption, by bribes and blackmail.

You do not address the issue of foreign relations in the original lecture. Can you indicate briefly the lines that a republican philosophy would support? And can you say how far the Zapatero government seems to have been following those lines?

The international order that a civic republican philosophy would recommend is one in which states that speak and act for their peoples, being democratically controlled in a suitable degree, are not subject to the domination of other states or of global bodies like multinational corporations and international agencies. If such states are dominated, then the citizens on whose behalf they speak are dominated too. These states should establish an order in which each enjoys freedom as nondomination and should seek to provide assistance for the members of oppressive and failed states; such states do not have a claim to freedom as nondomination in their own right, since this might not serve the cause of their members.

How might democratic states go about establishing an international order of mutual respect and external assistance? A first requisite is that relatively weaker states should combine in more restricted, multilateral associations to ensure that they make common cause against stronger states or against other bodies that would otherwise have an unchecked power of interference in their affairs, whether that interference be military, economic, or diplomatic in character. And a second is that, empowered in on this basis, they should combine in bodies where, as partners in dialogue, they authorize common values that can be invoked on all sides both to regulate their relations with one another and to organize initiatives on behalf of the members of oppressive or failed states.

This republican philosophy of international order is richer than the traditional philosophy that would only give states a right against active military intervention by other states and would ignore the sort of domination that does not require active intervention, military or otherwise, and that may derive from multinational corporations or agencies, not from states. But the philosophy is not so rich as to be utopian; in this respect it contrasts with calls for cosmopolitan equality or justice.

The performance of Spain over the past three years has been fairly true to the principles of the approach. The government has been a staunch defender of the United Nations and other such bodies, arguing for the importance of dialogue and the common understanding and action that this makes possible. A good example of its commitment on this front is the sponsorship with Turkey of the Alliance of Civilizations. It remains to be seen how far this venture succeeds but it is certainly the sort of enterprise that a good republican citizen of the world ought to be attempting. Again, the efforts that Spain has made in its relations with African and Latin American countries, as well as with Britain over the issue of Gibraltar, evince a commitment to dialogue of the same kind.

Has Zapatero's Spain displayed a recognition that despite its own power—it is now the eighth largest economy in the world—

the country needs to make common cause with other countries if it is to be safe against the power of multinationals and a country like the United States? I see some signs of its adopting the profile of a state that is willing to provide leadership among countries outside the G8 in international forums, but these are hard to read for sure. Within Europe, I see it as a state that is willing to help develop the culture of cooperation and compromise that is necessary if the European Union is to provide for its peoples. The strong-arm or stonewalling tactics that some European leaders are willing to adopt in the name of short-term national interests would undermine the capacity of the European Union in these regards, and it is noteworthy that from the beginning this government has avoided them. One area where common European action will be required, however, is in agreements to maintain corporate taxation levels, preventing multinationals from playing different countries off against one another. It is disappointing in this connection that Spain has followed a general trend in recently lowering its corporate tax.

Finally, I am pleased at the lead that Spain has given in raising its overseas aid by over 25% under the Zapatero government and in continuing to support United Nations peace missions. And indeed I was pleased at the decision to withdraw from the Iraqi adventure, since this was pursued without United Nations sponsorship and, as we now know—and as many argued in 2003—was not deserving of such endorsement.

Is the difference between freedom as nondomination and freedom as noninterference really substantial: really one of substance rather than of shadow, as Sr. Ramírez expressed it?

My overview of civic republicanism, contained in this volume, is designed to emphasize the points of contrast between the two approaches. Freedom as nondomination insists that, just to the extent that others control what I do in a certain choice, I am unfree, and it recognizes that others may control me without actually practicing or having to practice interference. Although they have the power to interfere as they wish, they may do so only when that is necessary to get me to behave according to their taste; they may let me follow my own inclination when that happens to fit with their preferences. If others have this power over me, of course, and I recognize that fact—as I normally will—then I may inhibit and censor my own behavior so as not to trigger their active interference. I will then serve as their agent in controlling myself so as to conform to their tastes; I will do their work for them.

There are two important implications of this approach for the understanding of freedom. First, it provides a rich goal for the behavior of the state in relation to its citizens. That goal is to equalize and increase people's freedom as nondomination in relation to one another, and in relation to outside agents or agencies. This explains why it is important for the state, to provide not just for the protection of its citizens, for example, but also for the empowerment of the more vulnerable.

The second implication of thinking of freedom in a control-centered way bears on how the state should organize itself rather than on the agenda that it should espouse in dealing with citizens. Suppose that others interfere with me but I control their interference, as with the interference my spouse practices when, with my blessing, she hides the cigars or the chocolate from me. Under the control-centered way of thinking, such interference will not reduce my freedom; it will not take away my control. This observation suggests that if the legislative interference of the state in people's lives is suitably controlled, then it will not be dominating. And so it identifies a goal for democratic and constitutional design: that of putting such institutions in place that the state's interference is as nonarbitrary or civically controlled as possible. I address that issue at some length in the overview essay.

Neither of these implications follows from the conception of freedom as noninterference. The goal of reducing interference is much more austere than the goal of reducing domination, since interference may be reduced without control and domination being reduced. And the goal of reducing interference says nothing about how the state should be organized, since the state itself interferes with its citizens whenever it legislates coercively, levies taxes, or imposes penalties. Thus proponents of the ideal of freedom as non-interference have always recognized that the ideal would support a benevolent despotism over a constitutional democracy, if such a despotism promised to do better in reducing overall interference (Paley 1825, 166; Berlin 1958).

4

AN INTERVIEW WITH
PRIME MINISTER ZAPATERO

PHILIP PETTIT, INTERVIEWER; TRANSLATED BY
JOSÉ LUIS MARTÍ AND JULIE SCALES

Prime Minister, I thank you for agreeing to this interview. I would like to begin with a general question. I understand that when you became leader of the opposition, you decided that you should articulate the general principles by which you would govern, if you won power. What prompted this decision to seek a general philosophy of government? Was it connected perhaps with the need to give the socialist or social democratic movement a new direction? Did you think that something more hard-edged was required than Tony Blair's rather vaguely defined Third Way?

I have always found ideas to be very important in politics, particularly for the Left. Even those who conceive of themselves as pure pragmatists actually have a conception of the world and a view of justice that are theoretical, even if they do not happen to know their intellectual origin. Their ideas originate in books, even if they have not read them, but are mediated almost unconsciously through the press, through debates, or merely through institutional shaping.

We, the socialists, are quite keen on debating about ideas. Indeed, when I became a member of the PSOE we were in the middle of a great ideological debate. It was 1979 and Felipe González had proposed that we renounce Marxism: our Bad Godesberg, twenty years after the German social democrats did it. At that time, I was eighteen and was following the whole debate with great interest. This all ended with the traumatic conference in which Felipe González resigned as leader of the party.

The truth is that we abandoned Marxism just when it was fashionable. Structural Marxism was about to undergo a deep crisis, a crisis that can be seen metaphorically in the dramatic endings of both Poulantzas and Althusser. I think Felipe was right; our party must not religiously embrace any doctrinaire position. Ideas are important, trends in thought are important, but only if we examine them critically, if we check them against experience.

Then, during the 1980s, the PSOE came into contact with the best of political liberalism, and people begin to read Rawls. I think this was a very fertile influence, one that we should not give up. It is true that some erroneously conflated political liberalism with economic neoliberalism; as today some mistakenly conflate civic republicanism with the rejection of monarchy. In any case, the PSOE adhered to a progressive and egalitarian liberalism in the 1980s, one decade before British Labour did.

For that reason it was paradoxical to me that, at the party conference where I was elected secretary general in July 2000, we were asked if we were going to follow Blair's way. We were the next generation of Spanish socialists, and were obliged to go beyond Felipe. And it was then, Professor Pettit, that you and your book *Republicanism* appeared in our history. It had been translated into Spanish just one year before, and we were reading it at that time. Your book clearly and systematically presents an old tradition of thought that is not foreign to us. Moreover, it has a practical side to it that I find extraordinarily useful for political work.

You eventually decided to take your guidance from the civic republican philosophy of government—on the model, broadly, that I tried to spell out in my 1997 book, Republicanism. *On that model, the central evil against which government should guard is the domination of citizens by other individuals or bodies. People will be dominated in this sense to the extent that they are controlled by others against their will, whether or not this control requires ac-*

tive interference. May I ask why this philosophy of nondomination
appealed to you? Did you think that the issue of domination was
already, implicitly, at the center of your concerns?

As I was telling you, the republican tradition is not alien at all to
Spanish socialists. There is an important group of young scholars
in Spain advocating civic republicanism, and one of them indeed
collaborates with you. And there are others who are not so young,
such as Salvador Giner, one of our intellectuals who has best cul-
tivated republican thinking. He was a disciple of Hannah Arendt,
who was one of the leaders of republican political thinking in the
twentieth century. Giner always insists on something I find very
important: maintaining the democratic tension in the republican
tradition.

But, in effect, freedom is the essential element. I have always
thought, since I was young, that personal freedom is the essential value of politics. Cervantes expresses the same in *El Quijote*:
freedom is the most valuable good, and it even worth risking our
lives for it. Freedom, the most valuable good.... The problem is to
which conception of freedom we are referring. And I agree with
you in that the ideal of freedom as nondomination is more demanding than the ideal of freedom as noninterference. Freedom as
noninterference is good for the one who lives alone on an island,
without others; but it is not enough for those who live in a polity,
in the presence of others.

Moreover, freedom as nondomination, that is, as nonarbitrary
interference, is more coherent with political activity, and therefore
is more coherent with regard to my own commitments, with my
vocation. I wonder what liberals want power for.[1] To be able to
do nothing? In the end, this is what constitutes their ideal: to not
interfere, to wait for the moment in which solely the blind forces
of the market fix everything. This could seem theoretically acceptable, but, in practice, in people's lives, there are no "blind forces,"
but forces with eyes wide open, trying to dominate others; forces
that sometimes have no problem putting people's health or even
the earth's health at risk. And, in this real context, the absence of

interference, the absence of laws and government, produces the same freedom that we see in the state of nature. This is why a conception of freedom grounded in laws, fair laws passed by democratic processes, seems more realistic to me.

So it is easy for a socialist to share a philosophy of nondomination, even more so when it is formulated as you do in your book. At the end of the day, you are the one who says that we need to formulate a gas and water republicanism, aren't you? In the same vein, democratic socialism is a gas and water socialism. It is a project of gradual reforms, reforms which effectively improve people's lives. We can increase people's freedom, and we can improve their well-being. But the two things work better if they go together. This is the purpose of my government's project.

Republicanism takes freedom to be a matter of nondomination and applies the ideal in the principle that government has a dual task. It should guard against the domination of citizens by other individuals or bodies and it should conduct its own business in a nondominating manner. Did you find that the ideal could be effectively invoked to explain this dual task and to make sense of your actions in government? Did people readily understand it? And was it possible to move and mobilize them on the basis of its appeal? I ask the question as someone who has thought a good deal about the idea of freedom as nondomination but who has never had to give it life in political debate.

In effect, once one acknowledges that political power is necessary, that government is necessary, that laws are necessary because all of them are the best guarantee for freedom, one should accept that this guarantee needs to be carried out. How should we use political power for making citizens more free? This is the relevant question. A liberal would agree that the best strategy is to reduce political power itself. But we already know that in practice nonpolitical powers emerge, and in a power vacuum, citizens tend to be left to the whims or interests of the powerful. We think that the combination of social policies and an enlargement of personal rights and liberties along with a reduction of arbitrariness in political power is the best strategy to guarantee nondomination.

To tell you the truth, I think that the great majority of Spaniards, a larger majority than those who vote for the PSOE, share the value of freedom as nondomination. People in Spain do not easily give up their freedom, perhaps because we recovered democracy not long ago. The most tragic, the harshest, but also the most enlightened, expression of what I mean is Spaniards' attitude toward terrorism. During the transition, the ETA's strategy was to provoke a coup d'état, by assassinating specific members of the military forces or the police. But the people did not demand an authoritarian reaction; they were opposed to any attempt at regression. Terrorism has not succeeded in instilling the fear among citizens that would be necessary to cause them to give up the guarantees of the rule of law; neither has it provoked them to fight against it, or defend themselves from it. I remember reading not long ago a CIS[2] poll in which 65% of Spanish citizens affirm that the government should not restrict individual rights under any circumstances. Even after Spain was brutally attacked by Islamic fundamentalist terrorism on March 11, 2004, there was not one sole act of xenophobia, not one demand for rights or liberties to be restricted. Spaniards love freedom, and do not like others taking it away, even if it is supposedly done for our protection.

Therefore, with this sort of citizenry, it is not difficult to start a project which aims to empower all citizens, men and women, in order to guarantee their freedom.

Ideals and principles, as you would be the first to emphasize, must always find expression in institutional designs and concrete policies. In this institutional spirit, republicanism has traditionally sought a regime that has a number of features: different centers of government have different, coordinated powers; the exercise of power is channeled by the rule of law and conducted in a transparent, dialogical manner; there is unlimited scope for ordinary citizens or their spokespersons to scrutinize and contest what government does or proposes to do; and these measures help to ensure that government adopts policies, and follows procedures, that fit with values that are endorsed across the community, not just in a particular class or coterie. I know that you are sympathetic to the need for each of these broadly democratic measures: the dispersion of power; the rule of law and dialogue; exposure to civic contestation; and responsiveness to common values. But do you regard them as equally important? Or do you tend to give priority to some over others?

All these elements belong to the same system. I do not know whether in theoretical terms it makes sense to put them in a hierarchy, but in practice the absence of any of them would make the political system unrecognizable. At least, this is certainly true in Spain, where territorial decentralization of power, for instance, fulfills a positive function. It encourages freedom with the vertical division of power: in this way we perceive freedom just as well as the founding fathers of American constitutionalism did. It also serves another function, which is equally important to our political integration: the recognition of the very territorial diversity which characterizes our country.

Of course, the perfection of a checks and balances system will always be crucial for freedom as well. This is a task that, even in a mature democracy (and I think that Spain in many respects is such a democracy), can always be improved. Thus, in this term we have increased the number of mechanisms that the opposition can use to keep the government accountable. For instance, the prime minister used not to appear before the sessions of the senate, and now I do. This is a precedent, and once a precedent is set, it is more difficult to turn back. The next prime minister will therefore have some problems if he or she tries to elude the senate's control.

Professor, before you asked me how certain ideals, such as dialogue or deliberation, can be put into practice. This term we have carried out important reforms to labor laws. We did it consensually, through dialogue among unions, employers, and the government. And it has been successful. It is no coincidence that we have had fewer labor conflicts during this presidency than in the history of Spanish democracy. The reforms of labor laws have been produced by agreement, and they are effective. We have decreased unemployment to the same levels as thirty years ago, to the levels we had previous to the oil crisis. It is true that some people proposed strategies taken from economics laboratories, but our experience tells us that the agreements born from dialogue are those that work better in practice.

In the same way, we have had a great deal of dialogue in parliament with the other political parties in order to build diverse majorities which enabled us to drive our reform agenda forward. Indeed, we have maintained a dialogue with all those who were willing to talk with us because we do believe in dialogue. What in Spain has been called *talante*, the good mood, has been a basic feature of the government of our rich, complex, and plural country, a truly essential element of our system.

The republican idea of dispersing power among many hands— the idea embodied in the traditional model of "the mixed constitution"—is often invoked in the United States and elsewhere as grounds for giving relative autonomy to different regional authorities. Was it the reason why you were open to the change in the statutes governing the relationship between the Autonomous Communities and the central government? Or was your willingness to increase the autonomy of those communities more a function of electoral demand and political incentive? Or was there perhaps an element of both concerns in your motivation?

This is related to what I just said regarding a necessary and absolutely basic feature of Spanish democracy: the vertical or territorial division of power. When the Spanish constitution was written, thirty years ago, there were no Autonomous Communities. Then, we could talk about them and design them in one way or another, according to a decision of the central power. Now it is not the same; the change is irreversible. The Autonomous Communities are mature political subjects with their own democratically legitimate power in a constitutional framework.

I think this is good because the experience of regional autonomy in Spain has been an absolute success, and I believe that the majority of the people would agree. The polls confirm, in effect, that Spanish citizens value the autonomy of their own regions and the state of the Autonomous Communities as a whole. Our experience is, then, a great example of the good of the ideal of the dispersion of power. It has been successful in several respects: in managing European funds, in managing our own resources, and so on. And here we have a modern and flourishing Spain, the result of a very dynamic democracy.

Our wish is obviously to pay attention to the Autonomous Communities' claims, whatever their political affiliation, whether they be governed by the right, the left, or the nationalists. This is because we have the firm conviction that our system works well and that it ought to be perfected thirty years after its beginning. But this conviction is not only ours. It is shared by political leaders of any ideology, not only in Madrid but elsewhere, since there are new subjects in politics which are the responsibility of the autonomous governments, subjects which did not exist thirty years ago. Now we cannot run Spain from its geographical center. This is history now, the history of our fathers.

In my review of your government I cited the common opinion that the Consejo General del Poder Judicial is a politicized body and does not have the independence we might expect under the principle that power should be dispersed and, in particular, that the judicial power should be separated from the legislative and executive. That politicization is due in part to the arrangement for appointing members that was introduced in 1985 by a PSOE government. Do you see the need or possibility for changing the basis of appointment to this body?

I do. For many the performance of the Consejo General del Poder Judicial (CGPJ)[3] over the past almost thirty years of the current constitutional regime is far from satisfactory from a constitutional standpoint. For, according to many commentators, this body constitutes an exception to the very positive balance of constitutional performance among the bodies and institutions regulated by the 1978 constitution.

This is possibly due to the fact that we have not known how to reconcile its two different objectives. On one hand, we are required to connect the election of CGPJ members with popular representation, in a transparent fashion according to the demands of a democratic state. This requirement applies because this is not a court or a judicial body, but the body of "government" of the judiciary. On the other hand, we have the no less important requirement of ensuring that the body serves an independent judiciary, with complete autonomy with respect to the other powers and branches of the state and other political bodies.

In these almost three decades we have had three different legislative models of nomination of CGPJ members, all of them within the framework of the constitution. And with all three we have felt the same dissatisfaction. All this leads me to think that the real problem is our collective lack of good democratic culture in the judicial branch, or rather, in the government of the judiciary. The greatest responsibility in fostering such a democratic culture is certainly in the hands of the two biggest political parties with chances to govern; but not all the responsibility is theirs: some of it belongs to the judges and their associations as well. I believe that I was aware of this and tried to act accordingly while I was the leader of the opposition, and I do so now as well in the governing party. But, honestly, I do not see the same constructive will in the main opposition party yet. Rather quite the contrary.

Notwithstanding, I would like to make one point clear. As it is set out in the law, the independence of judges and of all those who are in the judiciary in Spain does live up to the standards of developed democracies. Justice is independent in Spain even though the CGPJ, one of its instruments created by the constitution, has not found a pacific neutral institutional position in the realm of the state's highest bodies. We have, therefore, a pending task, but we also have to play down its real influence in the work of judges, the ones who are truly responsible for impartially adjudicating the law.

The republican idea of exposing governmental power to civic contestation requires ordinary people to be involved in the business of government, not just at election time, but also throughout the duration of a parliament. Popular engagement requires participation in referendums, even in demonstrations, as well as participation in local, professional, and consultative bodies. But do you think that it also requires engagement in social movements such as those that campaign for the rights of women, migrants, and consumers, as well as movements like Greenpeace and Amnesty International? Or do you see such movements as lobbies that push special interests rather than interests that government should rightly seek to favor.

Not only special interests, but special views too. In a society like Spain's, as in any other Western society, people live a very diverse and contradictory reality. If a particular industry sets up shop in my town, I benefit as a worker, but lose as an environmentalist. If a restaurant opens its doors in my own building, what benefits me as a consumer harms me as a neighbor because of the smells and noise. What is convenient to me as the parent of my child perhaps bothers me as a taxpayer. My desires as a driver are contradictory to my desires as a bike rider. From micro to macro, from everyday to global interests, there are contradictions not only among diverse social groups, but in the individual person's own interests.

Democratic politics entail deliberation, and deliberation has more quality when it includes all individuals, or associations, affected by any particular issue. In deliberation, when listening to the arguments made by others, we are capable of transcending, of elevating ourselves above our usual perspective. This is politics, the space of conflict and agreement, the place in which contradictory diversity can be accommodated in order to produce a more or less lasting harmony.

We have put a great deal of effort, for instance, into guaranteeing the presence of women in politics, but also in business. This does not mean that feminists are going to be able to impose their whole program, but it is then possible for them to explain and defend it. Exactly the same occurs with consumer associations, with immigrants, with environmentalists, and so on; they come to deliberate armed with their own perspectives, and this enriches the debate. Nobody, not even political parties, has a priori a complete vision of the general interests at stake. Such vision is built upon debate itself.

Are you concerned about the fact that, although there is a high propensity for popular demonstration, the engagement of Spanish people in social movements is low by European standards? Do you see any steps that government might take to improve this situation? Might government be able to sponsor and support social movements without taking them over, and thereby undermining their capacity to be independent sources of contestation?

I believe that the propensity you mention is valuable. Spanish citizens have expressed their commitment to general affairs whenever they found it necessary. The opposition to the Iraq War was a good example of Spaniards' civic commitment. Citizens pay more attention to what is going on in political life than is usually thought. In the past popular demonstrations seemed to be something characteristic of the Left, and the Right tended to be annoyed by them. But in this term the Right has made its own demonstrations, and I find it a healthy democratic exercise for them. I may disagree with their motives, but will never challenge their right to express them in a public demonstration.

On the other hand, it is true that scientific studies reveal that those countries that arrived later to democracy, such as Greece, Portugal, and Spain, have lower rates of social participation. This is an area where we should also emulate more developed democracies. When interests are organized, when they are clearly communicated, things are easier for everyone: for the people represented by them and for those who have to provide the necessary resources for solving problems. The problem is, again, a practical one. How do we do this?

The government of Spain, as well as the governments of the Autonomous Communities and the townships, has been promoting associations and social movements for years. And it is worth noting that at the local level new forms of participation and political engagement are always being tried. Furthermore, I am sure that new technologies will facilitate a greater connection between political leaders and the citizenry.

How much importance do you give to the education for citizenship that your government has introduced in the schools? Do you see it as helping to mobilize the young into becoming more engaged with government, in participatory or contestatory groups? Or do you think that it will have served its purpose if it at least generates a widespread appreciation of the importance of measures like those I mentioned: the dispersion of power, the rule of law and dialogue, the civic monitoring of government, and the responsiveness of government to community values?

All these measures are not incompatible, but rather they complement each other. And all of them are necessary. The path that we want to walk along is one of creation and development of a critical mature citizenry. A quality democracy is not content with a good institutional order. It also requires revitalization of such order, so to speak, with citizen participation and commitment: everyone should be aware of his or her own responsibility to it. One of the phenomena which contributes to trivializing democratic systems is the increasing individualism and privatization of huge sectors of the citizenry. Nowadays you can see how in many places consumers are more important than citizens. But it is necessary to take into account both dimensions of people. And following the civic republican tradition, I think moreover that being concerned about political issues enriches our person, and it is also a necessary condition for developed democracies to be well grounded. We need to attend to our civic duties as well as to our rights.

The subject "Education for Citizenship" may well contribute to awakening this dimension among children and young people. It is ideally intended to foster personal autonomy, while at the same time making us fully aware that we are beings with responsibilities toward others and toward the civic group to which we belong. It is, then, by definition, the antithesis of indoctrination. It is "education for freedom," both personal and collective, and I think it is essential in order to allow these children, in the long run, to make more independent political judgments as citizens. Having thoughtful citizens who are impelled to deliberate should be the ideal for all democratic systems. On this issue, as in many others, I feel close to Hannah Arendt and Jürgen Habermas. Let me tell you, Professor Pettit, that we are not inventing anything new here when we added this subject. We are simply following the path laid out by other big democratic countries in which it has been successfully introduced in schools.

The contestation of government is enhanced by media that are independent both of government itself and of special interests; if special interests are represented, then they should be given a balanced presence in different outlets. Do you think that the media in Spain live up to this standard? Are you happy with the performance of the national broadcaster now that it is responsive to parliament rather than to the government of the day? Has this change—a change of your own making—made life harder for you in government?

Today in Spain there are more media than four years ago. There are more TV channels, more newspapers, more digital news media … there is, in sum, more pluralism. We have, fortunately, a more robust marketplace of ideas. The appearance of more private media reflects Spanish society's own dynamism. The only things done by the government have been in the areas mediated by administrative decisions, such as the regulation of the new over-the-air (terrestrial) digital television, thus opening new pathways for this social dynamism, for this greater media plurality, instead of restricting them.

We have been sharp, decisive, and I think also conclusive, however, in regulating the state-owned public media. We have broken away from a sort of fatalism that had existed in Spanish democracy which consisted of using public media for the corresponding government's partisan interests. We committed to do it and we did it. Temptations are over. And I think that there is no going back. Citizens now would not tolerate it. And those Autonomous Communities, in which there has been abuse of the system, sometimes with a brazen lack of shame, will not be able to maintain this situation for long.

A ruler is forced often to make political decisions with ambivalent implications: decisions benefit some and harm others, they carry risks. But in this case the decision was univocal, clear, unquestionable. And when this happens, it is very difficult to claim credit for its success because now the alternative of keeping an instrument of unfair advantage like this in his favor, at the expense of the citizens, is not a viable option for a democratic leader in a political contest.

Turning to more specific matters, you have introduced a broad range of new policies and measures in the course of the past few years. These include the laws against gender violence, the law allowing homosexual marriage, the law of nondependency, the law of equality, and the measure whereby the position of over half a million illegal migrants has been regularized. I know you believe that these policies reflect political values of equality—equality in the enjoyment of freedom as nondomination—and that you take these to be implicit in the culture of Spanish democracy. But clearly many of them conflict with specific positions endorsed by the church and by other social groupings. Has this ever made you hesitate about taking the path you chose? After all, that path has generated very vocal and spirited opposition.

Taking into account my previous remarks, I do not believe that it is necessary to once again explicitly state the ethical-political foundation on which these policies are based, their source of legitimacy, which you also were referring to in your own question. I will focus then in my response on the second part of your question, the conflict that such measures may have generated, and whether they clash with the principles of institutions like the Catholic Church. The first thing I should say is that, perhaps with the exception of gay marriage, all the laws you mention have had not only wide social support, but great parliamentary acceptance as well. The laws against gender violence and the Dependency Act have been unanimously applauded and have been assessed very positively. There have been no problems with the Equality Act either, which plainly tells us that there was a wide social perception in Spain that something needed to be done. On the other hand, if we turn to the polls, 66% of Spanish people accept gay marriage. I consider these laws, therefore, not to be contrary to dominant values in Spanish society. And I include on the list all the measures taken in order to regularize the situation of illegal immigrants. Each and every one of these measures is well based on good reasons and has been persuasively defended in the public arena. This is not the case with the opposition, which has aggressively attacked two of them in particular: gay marriage and the measures for regularizing immigrants. They did so, in the first case, on the basis of moral considerations, and in the second by alleging that these measures were motivated by political opportunity. I will differentiate these two cases because my disagreement is also based on different criteria.

To begin with, here it is imperative to remember an essential aspect of the legitimacy of both initiatives: they were made necessary because of public ethical considerations and because of the demands of an inclusive democracy. A specific, particular moral discourse, like that of the Catholic Church, cannot claim the power to be the only possible foundation for public ethics. Let us consider our specific case. It does not seem legitimate to simply hypostasize their conception of family as the only possible one, especially in current times, in which this institution is undergoing a significant transformation. Defending this position does not mean, of course, as some have implied, that we are "attacking" the concept of family in order to give equal rights to homosexual and heterosexual people. Nor can it be argued that the measures for defending the family—such as those for large families—are no longer valid. The purpose of this law is to grant rights to those who historically have been deprived of them, without diminishing the rights of other groups. Putting it in terms of a zero-sum game is absurd and does not correspond to reality.

As for the measures to regularize illegal immigrants, they were required to grant rights, as well as obligations, to the hundreds of thousands of immigrants in our country illegally when we came into office. Leaving aside for now the responsibility of the previous administration, let us focus on what is really important. Would it not be a violation of all of our constitutional social rights if we denied them effectively to an important sector of our workers? How could we neglect the most basic personal dignity to those who participate and contribute to improve our country with their effort? I am sure we did what we ought to have done, as we do what we ought to when we resolutely favor legal immigration in our immigration policy, thus allowing to come to this country all those who can have a job here and integrate fully into this society, with legal rights and obligations.

I am sure you would say that political leaders ought to articulate values that they find in the community and ought to legislate and govern on the basis of those values; that is what makes them leaders, not followers. But it is also part of the job to make sure that people understand the basis in common values for the initiatives adopted by government. Do you see a need, in this connection, to run public campaigns for gaining recognition of the values behind your initiatives, for example, in favor of homosexuals, women, and migrants? Has enough been done by your government on this front?

One of the clearest assumptions of republicanism is the civic virtue of the citizenry. In contrast to liberalism, republicanism does not treat the ordinary citizen as politically handicapped. I am convinced that the laws we have passed correspond to the values of a majority of Spaniards. I believe in debate, in public deliberation, rather than in campaigns, in order to spread and better explain these values. But I insist: they are not imported values, but values already present in Spanish society.

It is true that some people on occasion are capable of distorting values, of defining tolerance as a weakness, the disposition to dialogue as a lack of personal ideas, the respect for the principles of living peacefully together as naïveté. This is our daily battle.

But another question is whether we have found our own place in the public sphere, which is most of the time bustling and vociferous, and are able to transmit the values in which our policies are inspired. In their essence, I think we have. Earlier we referred to how our measures to grant equality with women, gays, and immigrants have been applauded. Without a basic capacity for transmitting our discourse, their acceptance would not have been as far reaching in our society.

But I do not mind acknowledging that we have possibly not always been right in explaining the meaning of our measures. This is in part because of our sense of political decency, because we avoid spreading propaganda or tooting our own horn. The same modesty led us to promote legislation forbidding public financing of purely political propaganda campaigns about the administration's activities. This is a law which increases the quality of our democracy, and I hope it establishes among us an irreversible milestone, giving political leaders the duty of explaining our actions through the *regular* and plural democratic channels of political communication.

To return briefly to social movements, I wonder if you see a role for such movements in pressing and supporting the ends for which you enacted the progressive measures mentioned. The reduction of gender violence cannot be ensured by law or policing alone, according to many commentators, but only with the help of civic groups that are willing to support women in difficulty, to provide advice about their options, and to run refuges for those who actually suffer abuse. Do you agree with this? And do you think that government ought to facilitate, even help to finance, the operation of such groups?

In my opinion the idea of civil society has fortunately gained great importance and leads us to reaffirm the separation between the public and the private sector, between state and society, as something inherent to a constitutional state. But we should avoid exaggerating, as some intellectuals and social leaders are apt to do when they tend to form civic associations and to regard civil society in general as a new subject endowed with a sort of indisputable wisdom. In democracy you have formal political representation, which has been institutionalized in the better sense of the word. It defends the general interests of the citizenry, is subject to control and is accountable to public opinion. And then you can find associations, groups, and movements that legitimately embody certain values and local interests. The two worlds are fully complementary. The stronger the civil society, the better it provides stimulus for political representatives, arousing as a symptom of social vitality.

In the specific case you are referring to, it is particularly important for institutions to be able to rely on the support of associations and the media in order to fight against gender violence. I firmly believe in the importance of collaborating with movements in civil society in order to achieve our goals. We are doing so in a multitude of sectors, and the results are good. All our achievements in international cooperation, for instance, would have not been possible without their appropriate collaboration. German social democrats talk about the "activating state" to refer to the state's capacity to both "activate" and coordinate civil society at the same time. I openly support this idea.

I would like to move on now to issues of an international character. Spain under your government has been a very good European citizen, displaying a willingness to recognize the needs of other countries and to find common ground with them. But does this dialogical stance pay? It would certainly be appropriate in a deliberative community but sometimes the European community appears to be an arena where bullyboys are invariably the winners, at least in the short term. Opponents of your dialogical stance might argue that Margaret Thatcher, the current Polish prime minister, and indeed your predecessor as Spanish prime minister were more effective presences in the European system. What would you say to this criticism?

I am convinced of the importance of being a "good European citizen," as you have defined us. And this is so for two reasons. First, Spain sees itself as a country which is fully committed to the development of the European Union. This is why, as soon as we took office, we assumed the responsibility of aiding the European Union to avoid the risk of paralysis, as well as making the European institutions work perfectly well. For our vision of Europe, a Europe of citizens, it is essential that institutions work very well, since they are the main guarantor of citizens' interests. If we really want to build a Europe of citizens, in which they have a voice and are able to articulate their real problems, we as rulers need to give a good example by adopting attitudes of dialogue and consensus. This is why we tried to lead by example: not only have we been constructive partners of the Union, but, as you know, we were the first country to initiate a referendum about the draft of a new constitution in the European Union in order to give the citizens the opportunity to express their opinions about it. We are simply building Europe from Spain, and promoting our *modus operandi* of doing politics in its functioning. We are promoting politics based on consensus as well as respect of institutions and of the rules of the game.

The second reason why we have adopted a position open to dialogue is very simple: this is the more efficient for our own interests. What we did is give Spain back its credibility within the European Union as a constructive and reliable partner that believes in European goals. All those who know how the European Union works are aware that these are the best cards to play for a country to be able to achieve its goals in the long run. Our country's interests are better served by working modestly and constructively, thus allowing us to gain new allies, rather than being faced with futile confrontations which end up alienating allies that sooner or later you will need.

On the wider international front Spain has also been a good citizen, rallying behind the United Nations, championing the Alliance of Civilizations, opening up relations with African and Latin American countries, and setting a good example by the increase in untied, overseas aid. You and your government have displayed thereby a faith in the possibility of a multilateral world order in which peoples respect one another. Has your experience in govern-

ment sustained that faith or induced a certain degree of cynicism?
Do you still think of the initiatives you have taken as realistic
rather than utopian?

Honestly I can tell you that my experience has reinforced my
conviction that dialogue, within a framework of respect for international law, is the only sustainable way to solve problems among
peoples. Some do not seem to understand that we live in an inter-
dependent world in which many problems affecting our states are
global and can only be solved with global and multilateral mechanisms and reactions. When I talk about the need for multilateral
action, I am not expressing a preference for one kind of foreign
policy or another, but describing a reality: unilateral actions are
simply ineffective in the context of globalization.

Multilateralism is, furthermore, the best way to transmit the
concept of freedom as nondomination to the international sphere.
Multilateral mechanisms give voice and decision-making rights
to all the countries participating in the process, with the weakest
countries being granted an opportunity to defend their interests
that they would not enjoy otherwise.

Spain is totally committed to this multilateralist vision in its foreign policy. We are a country with a multilateralist vocation, open
to the world, with a capacity and a responsibility, derived from our
own history and identity, to serve as a bridge among peoples and
cultures. Thus, we have not only the will to contribute to effective
multilateralism, but also some "comparative advantages" which
place us in a privileged position to be able to play a significant
role in this field. I am referring to our history, geography, and national identity, which make us a diverse and tolerant country, with
a capacity to serve as a bridge between cultures and regions, and
allows us to be perceived as a "reliable mediator" in this field. We
also have some experience in the task of constructing democratic
institutions. We have some influence in the European Union as
well as in other regions such as Latin America. And we have at our
disposal all the economic resources generated by one of the most
prosperous and dynamic economies in the world. For all these reasons, Spain has a great potential capacity as an interlocutor. In our

current context, with some tensions among cultures, Spain has the responsibility of projecting this singular capacity of international dialogue.

This philosophy serves as a starting point for some of the multilateral initiatives you have mentioned. We have led by example, devoting some effort and resources to create mechanisms for allowing the countries and civil societies to solve their problems by negotiation and mutual understanding. I believe for that reason that our initiatives, far from being utopian, are viable and very necessary. We are idealists, but not naive. We are aware of the need to combine a dialogical attitude with resolution in defense of international law and of our interests when it is required. The current geopolitical context is complex and the only effective way of facing it is with a multidimensional set of policies to reach a sort of balance between pragmatism and the conviction that a better world is possible and we should try to create it. This is not easy, but it is essential. And I am convinced that by working for a better world we will become a better country, with an even more open and more solid identity.

One staple of republican wisdom is that different parties, whether they be individuals or governments, cannot seriously command one another's respect without each having a degree of power that guards them against the control or domination of others. This lesson clearly has relevance for the international world in which states differ enormously in resources and influence. What remedies do you see against the hegemony of powerful states, multinational corporations, or indeed global religions?

As I have explained, we find effective multilateralism to be the best way to give voice to the states in the weakest positions. Multilateral mechanisms avoid imposing "the law of the strongest," and allow design of win-win solutions. This is the first of the measures indispensable for avoiding the risks of abuse and domination: to foster the use of multilateral mechanisms.

But for these to be effective, we also need to create more and better institutions and mechanisms of global governance. As I said, many of the problems we currently face are global and can only be effectively managed through global mechanisms.

Third, we must still make further advances with regard to respecting international law. We, the progressives, believe in the existence of universal values and rights that respect cultural diversity, rights that we all are required to defend: life, freedom, and so on. In the last sixty years we have greatly improved the development of an international legal order that delineates these values and protects the inalienable rights that are founded on such values. But we should not let our guard down, and we should go further in our defense of international legal order since it is, to be sure, the most effective instrument to protect all people from abuses and domination.

Lastly, I think it is very important to mobilize the citizenry to take on this commitment. A world open to dialogue and peace is not possible unless we have a collective goal, a commitment of the citizenry to this vision of the relationships among peoples which requires their rulers to achieve mutual understanding through peaceful means. The goodwill of well-intentioned elite reformers is not enough.

Your government is planning to reduce the tax on large corporations from 35% to 30%, presumably because of the danger that commercial companies would otherwise relocate to countries with more attractive tax regimes. This signals a danger that powerful corporations may play states off against one another, even within the European community, and that they may induce a race to the bottom in which every country loses out and only the multinationals gain. Do you think that this is a danger? How would you propose to tackle it?

This is simply one of the many phenomena produced by economic globalization, and it is true that some of them engender uncertainty. But I think this involves a risk that can be minimized if we do things well.

Globalization is changing the rules of the game. And we should not fear the change, but take it as an opportunity, since the choice is not actually between change or status quo, but between managing the change in a productive way or being swept away by it toward a future defined by others. So the question is not whether we are for or against globalization, but whether we want this kind of globalization or another. The challenge is to manage it in such a way that we are able to combine an open attitude toward the opportunities of globalization with measures that grant freedom and (physical, economic, and cultural) security in the face of uncertainty.

To achieve this, it is fundamentally necessary to do two things. The first is pedagogical. For instance, we should not be alarmist in the particular case you refer to, tax cuts. Corporations tend to open their doors in countries that offer a good general economic environment. Tax policy is only one of the elements determining such an environment, and it is not the most important. If we are able to create a country, as we are doing, in which corporations find qualified workers, high levels of productivity, dynamism, and innovation, open and competitive markets, and so on, we will have no trouble attracting investment. I insist: what corporations want is for countries to be good partners for the long run, offering stability, competitiveness, and clear rules of the game. Indeed, you need only observe reality. In Europe we have higher tax rates than many other countries, but we are still the preferred destination for many corporations.

That said, it is true that we should reach consensus on some common rules of the game and then respect them. Based on our experience, all the members of the European Union already know that we all gain in the long run if we create a level playing field and all respect it. We must be alert in order to stop certain participants from abusing the power they receive from the new order. The best tools to avoid some people's vulnerability are effective laws to protect their rights and social policies to give them physical and economic security. For this it is essential to have effective public institutions. In other words, effective public action is one of the important conditions for achieving the goal of globalization as a source of wealth and progress, rather than one of instability and inequality. Thence, this is the significance behind defending the public and the role of institutions.

I have not asked you about problems in Spain that are of long standing and that your government has been trying, like its predecessor, to address; I am thinking of problems like those of educational dropout, lack of economic competitiveness, temporary contracts, and the slowness of the judicial system. But one problem I highlighted in my report was that of the overcrowded conditions under which prisoners must live. I highlighted this because I think that governments have little electoral reason to be concerned about prison conditions and that they need to be continually challenged on this front. Do you think the problem is serious? And how would you propose to deal with it?

We have increased our economic competitiveness, and the results of this increase will be still more visible in the next years, since we are making a considerable effort in research and development and infrastructure. Both things are essential for the future of Spain. We are also reducing temporary work contracts thanks to the agreements that have been reached between the government, the unions, and the employers. We have introduced reform legislation in education with the priority goal of fighting against school dropouts. During this term, we have created 1,000 new posts for judges and attorneys in order to make our judicial system more agile, although we still have much work to do in this field.

I share your concern about the problem of our overcrowded prisons. And I want to say that this is something I ask my advisors about frequently. I would like to tell you my own experience as prime minister. A ruler is usually concerned about providing citizens with good service of public safety. In this term, we have hired 15,000 new police officers, and we have one of the lowest rates of crime in developed countries (19 points below the European mean). But I have also looked at the other side of the coin, at the situation of our prisons, since two things are required for a minimally sensitive democratic leader: to fight effectively against crime, this abominable domination of freedom, particularly against all sorts of moral or physical assault, and also to rely on a prison system which is able to attend to the needs of its prisoners, and to fulfill its rehabilitative function. As prime minister, I feel constitutionally obliged to achieve both ends.

It is true that our prison system is partly overcrowded. My government has been concerned about this problem and is taking measures to alleviate this situation. When we took office, prison population had grown almost 30% in the previous four years, but only four new penitentiaries were scheduled to be built, and ground had not yet been broken. At the end of 2005 we launched an ambitious plan for creating new penitentiaries, which supposes an almost 200% increase in the prison infrastructure budget, if we compare with 2003.

We are taking, then, significant steps to balance the situation, and we are doing so because, in effect, we consider it a political obligation that appeals to our sense of responsibility as a government.

And now a last question. Would you recommend to fellow leaders in the European Union and elsewhere that they pay attention to the civic republican tradition? I do not mean pay attention to my book in particular but to the tradition that it tries to articulate for contemporary purposes. And if you would recommend this, what sorts of considerations would you adduce in support?

I do see interest on the Left, from European democratic socialism, in civic republicanism, even when sometimes it is not conscious of this. The truth is that the Left is interested particularly in politics; we want it as an instrument of transformation, reform, and perfection of our societies. And republicanism is a good vindication of politics and its value. This is a very clear difference with the Right; at least this is obvious in the Spanish case.

The democratic Left is already aware of the room for action left by the economic and social model. The social state is not governed in the same way, to be sure, by liberal conservatives or by social democrats. And we also see this in Spain. But perhaps politics, the possibility of creating better societies with stronger and freer citizens, is at stake above all in other arenas: in the areas of rights, of media pluralism, of democratic pedagogy, of the institutional reforms, and so on. All these are aspects enriched by the view of civic republicanism.

So, yes, I conceive of myself as an advocate for it. I frequently talk about its contribution with my colleagues in other countries, especially with progressives. And the arguments are, to a great extent, the same as those outlined throughout this interview. The Left needs to reflect on politics, on how to improve the quality of politics, on institutions, and also on its own partisan organizations as well. The requirement of civic values, of being involved with the fate of others, the reaction against domination, the drive for a deliberative democracy, all are topics in which the Left is more and more interested, and which all belong to this long tradition of political thought.

5

GIVING PHILOSOPHY
A PUBLIC LIFE

PHILIP PETTIT AND JOSÉ LUIS MARTÍ

THERE ARE MANY REASONS to favor the exercise whereby a philosophy is given the role in public life that civic republicanism appears to have played in Zapatero's Spain. The most important, by our own lights, is provided by the civic republican consideration that people will be better able to invigilate and control government—better able to implement a contestatory form of democracy—to the extent that that government commits itself, not just to a hodgepodge of policies, but to a unified philosophical outlook. We expect a political philosophy to have a public role both in offering guidance in institutional design and governmental decision-making and in offering direction to citizens in the public exercise of deliberation and contestation.

If a philosophy is to be capable of playing such a role in public life, however, then it will have to meet suitable design specifications. Not just any philosophy will be able to play the part required. In this last chapter we provide an analysis of the most important conditions that have to be satisfied; we look at how those conditions are often breached by political philosophies; and we argue that civic republicanism does particularly well in meeting them.

While we concentrate on the extent to which political philosophies can play a part in public life, we do not mean to suggest that that is the only function they should serve. Political philosophers pursue many abstract studies that have little direct connection to public life, including exercises in conceptual analysis, institutional theory, formal modeling, and intellectual history, as well as thought experiments in the demands of perfect justice. We are ourselves invested in such studies, often from a civic republican standpoint, and we see great intellectual value in their pursuit.

The assumption behind the exercise of this chapter, however, is that, no matter what tasks it discharges in those more abstract domains, a political philosophy should identify an ideal or set of ideals that it takes to be important for government to foster and exemplify. And we hold that on this front—at this bottom line—it should strive to be capable of serving in a public role. A philosophy that concentrates on other tasks such as the identification of what perfect justice requires may be capable of serving in a public role as well (Martí 2006; Estlund 2009); and a philosophy that can serve in a public role may also be able to discharge others tasks too—indeed we think that this is true of civic republicanism. In the argument of this chapter, we make a priority of the capacity for public service and ask what it requires of a political philosophy. What are the features that would enable a political philosophy to play a useful public part and reach the hearts and minds of citizens as a whole?

We think, broadly, that three conditions are important. First, the ideal or set of ideals advanced must be able to be shared equally among the members of the polity: it must be universally accessible and acceptable, so that there is no block to people's endorsing it as an organizing principle of their common life. Second, the ideal has to be realistic in the assumptions it makes about people's motivational and cognitive capacities: it must be manifest that the ideal is not too demanding to be capable of being realized and upheld. And, third, the ideal must have an energizing capacity such that we can expect it to command the affection and allegiance of ordinary people, challenging them to look for improvements in their social and political life and guarding them against complacency or indifference.

Our discussion in the chapter will be structured around these three conditions. We will discuss in turn what is required for a political ideal to be shareable, realistic, and energizing, and after each discussion we will state the claims of the civic republican ideal to satisfy the condition discussed.

A Shareable Ideal

The Condition in General

Given a particular polity or regime, an ideal will be shareable there insofar as relevant individuals can equally give it countenance and importance. But who are the individuals who count when we try to determine if an ideal meets this condition? There are two extremes to avoid, one elitist, the other cosmopolitan. The elitist extreme would limit the enfranchised category to a privileged subgroup, whether the privilege be one of race or birth, religion or gender. The cosmopolitan extreme would extend it to all those individuals, including the members of other states, whose fates are likely to be affected by the polity. The elitist view is democratically objectionable, the cosmopolitan manifestly infeasible. We choose a middle path.

We assume that the relevant individuals should be equated with all the adult, able-minded, permanent members of the polity, however precisely the thresholds of age and ability and residence are set. Those individuals should be given an equal chance to speak, and an equal hearing, within the polity: an equal opportunity to contribute to the public deliberation. And an ideal will count as shareable only to the extent that it can be given the same countenance and importance across their ranks as an ideal for ordering collective policy. There is nothing about the ideal that makes this impossible, difficult, or unlikely.

If an ideal is shareable among the sort of citizenry we envisage, then a first requirement is that it not be sectional or factional, serving only the interests of a particular subgroup. It was a concern to avoid this particular problem that led Aristotle to hold that all the true or incorrupt forms of government, be that government monarchical, aristocratic, or democratic, had to focus on the common good or the public interest. The notion of the common weal gives us the word "commonwealth," for long a name for a legitimate state that operates with a view to the welfare of the whole.

What might be an example of a sectional ideal? In particular, what might count as an example among the ideals that are likely to be proposed as determinants of public policy in a contemporary democratic system? The most plausible example may be the unicultural, perhaps nationalist, ideal that we can imagine being held up as a guiding beacon in a society where there are minority cultures associated with indigenous or immigrant peoples. The high-flown rhetoric of unity and nationalism can provide a mask for presenting as a universal ideal something that answers properly only to the interests of a subpopulation—usually, a dominant subpopulation—not to the shared interests of the whole.

But being sectional is not the only way in which an ideal can fail to be shareable equally by all. It may also fail through being sectarian. Where an ideal will be sectional to the extent that it privileges the interests of a subgroup in the society, it will be sectarian to the extent that it privileges ideas that are held only by the members of a subgroup, not by people across the society. It gives priority to the opinions, if not the independently determined interests, of that particular class.

The most straightforward example of this failure of shareability is provided by the case where the views of a religious majority or minority are given a special standing in the determination of political policy. We are familiar with this particular failure from the many cases where formally or informally entrenched churches manage to impose their views in particular areas of policy. In Western countries these views, more often than not, bear on moral matters, in particular moral matters related to procreation and marriage. In other societies, as in Western societies at an earlier time, they extend to views on the status of religious authorities and the role they should play in the decisions of government.

Apart from sectional or sectarian ideals, there are ideals that are unshareable because of having a sectional or sectarian effect in the context where they are proposed. They are contingently sectional or sectarian, and usually covertly so. They have an objectionable effect, not as a matter of their inherent character but rather as the result of a contingency of the context where they are applied.

Here the outstanding example is the ideal embodied in the majoritarian principle of decision-making: what's best in any area of policy is what answers best to the preferences or judgments of the majority. This principle might count as egalitarian—nonsectional and nonsectarian—in a society where public issues of the same importance attracted different majorities and everyone could reasonably expect to have an equal chance of being in the majority on any issue. But that sort of society hardly exists under normal sociological conditions, where cleavages tend to be relatively firm and unchanging. Under such conditions the majoritarian ideal will be not be equally shareable among members of the society. Let the majority be those of a distinctive race or religion, for example, and the ideal will be indistinguishable from the overtly sectional or sectarian ideal of giving that race or religion a privileged status in the shaping of policy. There is nothing wrong in the majoritarian principle per se, but under such conditions it can have a sectional or sectarian effect.

Are there other examples of covertly sectional or sectarian ideals? The utilitarian and economic ideal of maximizing preference-satisfaction will have this character, when the distribution of actual preferences means that maximizing their satisfaction will play in favor of one group. For a vivid example from the international rather than domestic context, consider the memo by Lawrence Summers, then chief economist to the World Bank, which was leaked in 1991. This made a case for exporting heavy polluting industries to the third world on the ground, roughly, that the antipollution preferences of poorer, shorter-lived individuals would not be as strong as those of the richer and longer lived. The memo caused indignation worldwide, because it so clearly gave an advantage to those in the more developed part of the world. A Brazilian official wrote in understandable incredulity that the reasoning was "perfectly logical and totally insane."[1]

The Shareable Republican Ideal

Is the republican ideal of freedom as nondomination unshareable in any of these ways? It is not a sectional ideal, because it does not put forward the interests of any particular group; it hails a value that encompasses the interests of people generally. It is not a sectarian ideal, because the value it hails is one with ecumenical appeal: one with an appeal that does not depend on adherence to any particular sect or ideology. It is, in both these respects, an ideal of the common good.

Are there contingent considerations why the promotion of the republican ideal would work to a covertly sectional or sectarian effect? Like any other political philosophy, republicanism may be used hypocritically—perhaps even self-deceptively—so as to conceal such interests, serving as a means for ideological manipulation. But the case is very different from the example of majoritarianism or utilitarianism. By contrast with such philosophies, there is no inbuilt feature that makes republicanism serviceable in a sectional or sectarian cause. On the contrary, it will take some effort to argue for such a cause on the grounds of freedom as nondomination for all.

Critics of republicanism, especially critics of a libertarian stamp, might argue that freedom as noninterference appeals on a more universal basis than freedom as nondomination, because it is less demanding. Does this make it into less than an ecumenical ideal: an ideal that should be acceptable on all sides? We do not think so.

The best way of making a case for the ecumenical character of freedom as nondomination is to show that, unlike freedom as noninterference, it counts in John Rawls's (1971) sense as a primary good. A variety of freedom will count as a primary good if it is the sort of thing that people are each likely to want for themselves, no matter what else they want. It is a valuable possession, no matter what their ends or purposes; it is a multipurpose or, better, an omnipurpose good. Freedom as nondomination has this omnipurpose character, freedom as noninterference does not. It may or may not count as intrinsically valuable but it will be instrumentally valuable for any agent, or at least for any agent with ends that are not inherently self-frustrating or self-defeating.

Freedom as nondomination is an omnipurpose good, because any shortfall will put you to some extent in the hands of others, giving them a certain control over your choices, and this forcible exposure to others—this dependency on their goodwill—is bound to raise a question as to what you can hope to achieve in action. It will mean that you lack the *sui juris* status associated with freedom in the Latin legal tag; you will not be wholly your own person. You will live on some front, in some measure, *in potestate alieni*: in the power of another. And so you will not be able to advance your own goals, just as you will. No matter what those goals are, therefore, you are liable to want the standing vis-à-vis others that goes with having freedom as nondomination. You will want freedom in the sense of the eighteenth-century republican text, Cato's letters: "Liberty is, to live upon one's own terms; slavery is, to live at the mere mercy of another" (Trenchard and Gordon 1971, vol. ii, 249–50).

The same cannot be said about freedom as noninterference. Suppose you live under the shadow of a power of interference on the part of others. And imagine that you are required to take whatever steps will provide you with the best expectation of noninterference. The steps required may be to self-censor your options, so as not to make a choice that is likely to trigger the interference of others. Or perhaps to ingratiate yourself with the others, so that you can manipulate them into having a taste for giving you free rein. Is freedom of noninterference, procured on such a basis, likely to be something you would want, no matter what else you want? Of course not. The servility and self-evacuation involved in taking such steps will not appeal to anyone who cares, as most of us do care, about being able to act without having to seek the grace or leave of others. In the scenario involved you would be reduced to acting only *cum permissu*, in the old republican phrase: only on condition that it pleases those with power in your life.

We conclude that not only does freedom as nondomination encompass the interests of people generally in a society and not only does it have a robust appeal across variations in the status quo;

it is also an ecumenical ideal that, unlike freedom as noninterference, represents an omnipurpose good: something that each of us must want for ourselves, no matter what else we want. But, if this is right, then how could someone like Isaiah Berlin, and the many who took his lead, argue so forcibly for the attractions of freedom as noninterference? Our sense is that, while Berlin always framed his views in terms of noninterference, he didn't ever see and embrace what it literally required. This appears in the fact that he never recognized that, if noninterference is what matters, then self-censorship and self-ingratiation need not be objectionable. On the contrary, the metaphor he used to express his image of freedom was one in which the prospect of such self-evacuation had no place. A decade after the appearance of his 1958 article, he wrote: "The extent of a man's negative freedom is, as it were, a function of what doors, and how many are open to him; upon what prospects are open; and how open they are" (Berlin 1969, xlviii; also xxxix).

The doors metaphor already takes Berlin halfway to the republican ideal of freedom, since it means that self-censorship cannot secure freedom. All doors must be open, he thinks: it is not enough that you happen to select, or plan to select, only the particular doors that are. The metaphor would have taken him the full republican distance if he had only recognized that not only must all the doors be open, not only must no doors be locked or jammed, there must not be any doorkeepers present whose goodwill you have to procure or maintain if the doors are to remain open. The republican ideal of enjoying freedom in a particular sort of choice can be perfectly well expressed with the help of this metaphor. The doors that represent different options—even options you are unlikely to choose—must ideally be open. And, ideally, there must be protections available which mean that there are no doorkeepers, not even any generally benevolent doorkeepers, who are in a position to close those doors, should they will. You will enjoy freedom as nondomination in the choice—you will be not be subject to uncontrolled interference, invigilation or intimidation—just to the extent that those conditions are fulfilled (Pettit 2008d).

A REALISTIC IDEAL

The Condition in General

The first, shareability condition that a philosophy must fulfill if it is to play a role in public life, in governmental decision-making and popular contestation, is one that we might expect any appealing political philosophy to satisfy. The second condition, however, is different. It requires that a philosophy that aspires to such a guiding role should identify an ideal that is not out of reach in ordinary circumstances. It does not presuppose a heroic motivation that is in short supply among human beings and it does not impose excessive cognitive expectations.

There are many appealing political philosophies that may not meet this condition. They might put forward an ideal of perfect justice, for example, or an ideal of the sorts of arrangements we might be able to attain if only such and such motivational or cognitive limitations did not apply. Such philosophies will give us a foil by which to judge the actual, as models of the perfectly competitive market provide a foil by which to judge actual markets. And they may serve to energize us better than some philosophies that are tailored more closely to what we are capable, in our imperfection, of achieving. We turn to the energizing issue in the next subsection, arguing for its equal importance with the condition of realism. But nonrealistic philosophies will not be able to play the directive role that we are assuming for a philosophy in public life. They will provide us with broad, orientating ideals, not with ideals for the guidance of government or citizenry in the conduct of day-to-day public life.

In his *Social Contract*, Jean-Jacques Rousseau set out to take human beings as they are—that is, to take human beings in all their motivational and cognitive imperfection—and to look at laws as they might be. Immanuel Kant sought in similar terms to look at what might plausibly be built in social and political life, working with the crooked timber of humanity. The requirement that a public philosophy put forward a realistic ideal or set of ideals can be cast as one that is broadly continuous with this sort of approach. In terms that economics has made familiar, the ideal proposed should be compatible with the incentives that actually move human beings—and, we must add, the cognitive limitations that they actually display (Brennan and Pettit 2005).

The motivational aspect of the realistic-ideal constraint is the most familiar, possibly because of the economic insistence on the need for incentive compatibility. The idea is that a public ideal should not be one whose institutional realization depends upon a robust degree of virtue among the members of a society, in particular among the authorities. Behind the proposal is the assumption that human beings are not all reliably virtuous or public spirited, or at least that such virtue is in short or uncertain supply. Let an ideal presuppose public virtue and the attempt to institutionalize it may flounder in the presence of less savory motivations. And that sort of failure may leave the society in a worse position than it would have been in had the experiment never been tried. Seeking the best may be inimical to achieving the good; it may lead to a third-best rather than a second-best result (Martí 2006, 26–31).

The lesson derived from the motivational constraint is that in selecting ideals, and in seeking out the institutions by which to realize them, we should economize on virtue (Brennan and Hamlin 1995). We should rely on the presence of a measure of virtue that looks likely to be available, and on the presence of such a measure only.

This constraint should not be confused with the so-called knave's principle: that is, with the recommendation that we assume that people are generally corrupt, lacking any degree of public spirit. Bernard Mandeville (1731, 332) put that principle in circulation when he looked for a dispensation that "remains unshaken though most men should prove knaves." Not content with a refusal to rely on people's being generally virtuous, Mandeville would have us assume—implausibly, as we think—that they are generally knavish.

Even if people are not knavish it may seem prudent to assume such a lack of virtue when we seek to identify political ideals that are institutionally sustainable (Brennan and Buchanan 1981). This, however, would be a mistake, as a body of empirical literature has begun to make clear. Put checks and sanctions in place that assume people will generally fail to be virtuous and there is a real danger that they will act to that pattern, whether out of defiance or demoralization or a variety of such responses (Grabosky 1995; Braithwaite 1997; Frey 1997; Frey and Jegen 2001). Design institutions that can survive "though most men should prove knaves" and you may end up designing a social world in which people generally prove to be knaves.

We interpret the motivational constraint in a less radical spirit. We think that it argues against presuming widespread virtue in practice, and that it requires us to be on our guard against the appearance of corruption. But we believe that it argues equally for building on—and if possible, developing—whatever virtuous motivation proves to be present. We would follow such a strategy, were we to rely in the first place on constraints of shame and honor (hypocrisy, after all, is the tribute that vice pays to virtue) and only use sanctions of a more punitive sort as a second or third resort. That strategy would fit with the traditional republican assumption that people are corruptible rather than corrupt and that they can be channeled or maintained in the ways of public virtue within a suitable economy of esteem (Brennan and Pettit 2004). The traditional mantra is that all power corrupts, the assumption being that people come to power with a modicum of public spirit still intact. And the traditional remedy has been to assume that within a suitable culture people's love of honor and fear of shame can be relied upon to keep them on virtuous paths and, ideally, to push them to higher levels of virtue (Pettit 1997, chap. 7).

So much for what is required in order for a political ideal to be realistic in its motivational assumptions. But an ideal might be motivationally realistic without being realistic in the assumptions it makes about people's cognitive capacities. There are two respects in which an ideal might offend on this front. It might require ordinary people to have a level of understanding that is not commonly attainable. Or it might require the experts or authorities in a political system to have an exactness of insight, or a wealth of information, that is often too hard to come by. If these limitations are only contingent then it may be important to look for institutions in which they are overcome. But to the extent that they cannot be overcome, a philosophy that hopes to play a full role in public life must not assume them away.

It is crucial that the officials within a political system have the cognitive wherewithal to target and pursue any ideal they are charged with implementing, so it is clear on this side why a political ideal has to be cognitively realistic. But a parallel argument shows why the ideal has to be cognitively realistic from the viewpoint of ordinary people as well. People will play a part in implementing any ideal, complementing the efforts of the authorities, insofar as it is they who are best at spotting failures of realization and making corresponding complaints (McCubbins and Schwartz 1984). If the ideal is cognitively too taxing for them to be able to track it, then that is going to make trouble for its reliable implementation. The point is bound to resonate strongly within a civic republican frame, due to the insistence there on the need for an invigilating, contestatory public. If the price of liberty is eternal vigilance, then liberty had better be an ideal that all can understand and identify.

There is no shortage of ideals in political philosophy that are motivationally unrealistic, requiring monastic restraint or comradely self-sacrifice. But what sorts of ideals violate constraints of cognitive realism? A good example, we think, is Rawls's ideal under which two principles would rule in society. First, there should be a system of maximal, equal liberty for all; and, second, there should be a regime that allows material inequalities just when they emerge under fair equality of opportunity and, as in a trickle-down effect, make the worst-off better off than they would be in any alternative (Rawls 1971, 1993, 2001).

These principles have many attractions but they run into a serious problem on the cognitive front. For it is unclear how those in charge in a society are going to be able to keep up with the evolving effects of policy in order to ensure that the second principle is reliably realized. How are they to determine who the worst-off is? If they can determine this, how then can they determine that the worst-off is better off than the worst-off counterparts under rival ways of organizing things? And if this is a problem for those in command, it will be a more serious problem still for those whose role is to monitor and contest policy-making. How are they supposed to tell whether this sort of ideal is being sincerely pursued or successfully implemented?[2]

One of Rawls's harshest critics was Robert Nozick (1974), who also pressed the difficulty of implementing a principle that, in his phrase, would have to limit capitalist acts among consenting adults. But Nozick's own libertarian recommendations also fall foul of cognitive realism. He argues for a laissez-faire system in which private property rights are extended maximally over the domain of the ownable and, subject to an ultraminimal state, distribution is determined by free market choice. In effect, he suggests that the presumptive principle of social life is that no one, the state included, ought to interfere in domains where others hold property and related rights and that the ultraminimal state is allowable only insofar as it represents an arrangement that rational people would be led to invent, did it not already exist.[3] Nozick argues, reasonably, that this system can only begin to have appeal if it embodies procedures for rectifying past injustices in the appropriation of property. But at that point the ideal, like Rawls's, runs into conflict with ordinary cognitive limitations. For how on earth could we hope to identify relevant injustices, trace their effects through subsequent transmissions of property, and then concoct suitable forms of rectification?

The Realistic Republican Ideal

Apart from being fully shareable among the members of a polity, the republican ideal of nondomination also has the virtue of being realistic in both its motivational and cognitive presuppositions. The motivational hold of the ideal stems from the fact that, because it is a primary good, freedom in this sense is something that everyone is likely to seek and cherish. People may not be familiar with the idea of nondomination or may not be used to associating it with the notion of freedom, but they cannot fail to recognize and resonate with the condition that the idea identifies. Everyone knows what it is to be under the thumb of another, required to seek leave or secure the other's good grace before being sure of having the ability to pursue one or another goal. And people who know this are bound to treasure the condition in which such dependency on the goodwill of others is absent and they can behave as their own men or women.

The universal familiarity with domination shows up in the wealth of idiom and metaphor that has been coined to describe it. There is a long tradition in English, for example, of denouncing a subservience to others that requires you to toady or fawn or kowtow, to bend the knee or doff the cap or tug the forelock, to placate or ingratiate or seek the good graces of one's betters, to live in servitude and servility. Raised in such a language and culture, you cannot fail to register the distaste that such a prospect merits. More positively, you cannot fail to be attracted to the alternative scenario in which you can walk tall, and look others in the eye, conscious of being recognized as someone who commands respect and enjoys equal status with the best.

But this is just to argue, of course, that everyone is bound to register the appeal of freedom as nondomination in his or her own life. Does it follow that they will register its appeal as a universal value: an ideal for people in the society as a whole? We think that this does follow, under the assumption that collective, political life is a natural necessity, not something that people can choose to leave, and that in conducting this life together, they have no defensible option but to treat each other as equals and to identify and invoke an ideal that all can share together. If it is possible for people to achieve this sort of life together, then it must be possible for them to recognize the appeal to others of what appeals to them and, affirming the equal hearing that each commands, to orient their efforts together around the promotion of freedom as nondomination for all.

In articulating what this means, we have a choice between two models. We may imagine that people are capable of escaping their own narrow perspective and embracing the cause of freedom as nondomination for all. Or we may think that, while they remain firmly attached only to their own freedom as nondomination, they are capable of recognizing that they can call on a collective state to protect this personal good only to the extent that they are willing to have it protect the counterpart good for each member of the society. We need not judge which of these scenarios, or which mix of scenarios, is likely. We just think that there is no extravagance involved in supposing that people can be motivated around a common value of freedom as nondomination for all.[4]

This is a particularly modest assumption, given that we are allowed to assume that, while people are corruptible, they are not necessarily corrupt. This means that we may hope to reinforce the natural inclination to embrace the common value of freedom as nondomination by relying on constraints like those associated with the economy of esteem. Suppose we publicize the standards of behavior that the republican ideal requires in public life, whether on the part of authorities or of ordinary citizens. And suppose we arrange things so that breaches of those standards are likely to become matters of common awareness. The prospect of shame that attaches to such a breach will affect anyone who cares about being taken to be virtuous: that is, taken to be attached to the publicly promulgated standards. And so it ought to provide a means—a first line of defense against corruption—whereby the motivational requirements of the republican ideal are more or less assured of fulfillment (Pettit 1997, chap. 7).[5]

So much for the motivational realism of the ideal. But how does it fare on the cognitive side? Is the ideal of freedom as nondomination more realistic than Rawls's principles, for example, in its presuppositions about the cognitive capacities of human beings? We think it is.

The problem with Rawls's principles is that it is unclear how authorities or ordinary citizens would be able to determine that those principles were satisfied. But there is no comparable difficulty with freedom as nondomination. If this ideal is less than fully satisfied in a society, then that means that some individuals are unable to achieve the walk-tall, look-in-the-eye status that we associate with enjoying nondomination. If some individuals are lacking in this way, then that is going to be obvious both to them and to those who deal with them. The imbalance of power that induces such a dependency is going to be there for all of us to see, and given that it is something that matters deeply to each one it is going to be something that we cannot fail to register.

But it is one thing to be able recognize that there is a shortfall in the freedom as nondomination that people enjoy in a polity. It is another to have the ability to recognize that, as between two possible scenarios of less than full freedom as nondomination, one is better than the other. Is the republican ideal likely to face problems on this front?

We freely acknowledge that for many variations in the imperfect realization of freedom as nondomination, it is not going to be possible to say which is better than the other. But that will often be because there is no determinate fact as to which is better, as there may be no determinate fact as to whether one person is balder or fatter than another, or enjoys greater satisfaction or better health. The ideal is vague in the relevant range—the range, as we say, of borderline cases—as any system-level political ideal is likely to be vague. That range need not be large, however, and where there is plausibly no such vagueness in play, where, intuitively, one scenario is decidedly better than the other, there is every reason to expect that the superior one will be identifiable. We will be able to say that this or that scenario is worse than another because more people suffer a similar deficit in freedom as nondomination, or because the deficit they suffer is more serious: it affects intuitively more important choices.

To conclude, then, we see no reason to think that the republican ideal of freedom as nondomination is less than realistic in either its motivational or cognitive aspects. It represents a condition that everyone is bound to care about in his or her own case and, under the requirements of collective life, to authorize as a common focus of concern. And it represents a condition to which everyone is sufficiently sensitive to be able to monitor the level of its realization and the ways whereby it may be best increased. To embrace this ideal and to hail it as a beacon of social and political life is not to forsake realism about human nature but to work safely within the parameters of what is socially and institutionally possible.

AN ENERGIZING IDEAL

The Condition in General

No matter how shareable and how realistic, however, a political ideal will be worth very little if it does not retain a capacity to lift people's eyes from the status quo and to inspire them with a vision of a better life. In logic there may be a time and place when no possibilities of improvement remain open but in practice it is never going to come; the way things are will always fall short of the way they might and would better be. And so it is important that a political ideal not allow people to settle complacently for the status quo, congratulating themselves on what they have achieved and neglecting to think about how they might still do better. This is not to recommend sustained instability or permanent revolution but only to caution against premature sclerosis of the political imagination. Let an ideal be in danger of inducing such sclerosis and it will have failed an important desideratum.

The desideratum, as we express it here, is that a satisfactory political ideal should be robustly energizing. It should serve in any real-world scenario as a regulative ideal that guards people against untimely satisfaction with how things are and that guides them in the search, often incremental and unromantic, for ways of bettering the world. But what are the characteristics of an ideal that are likely to give it a suitably energizing character? We can think of at least five. A political ideal will be more energizing to the extent that it is a broad ideal that encompasses different aspects of institutional design, policy-making, and civic action; a deep ideal whose pursuit ensures against a variety of ailments in social life; a robust ideal that has lessons to teach about how to make things better, even when perfection is a distant prospect; an ideal that respects the personal sphere, acknowledging the limits of what a coercive state may achieve; and an ideal that engages with actively avowed complaints and is capable of gripping hearts as well as minds.

A BROAD IDEAL

An ideal will be broad to the extent that it carries constitutional lessons for how the state should be organized as well as substantive lessons for what it should try to do. Many richer political philosophies, among them utilitarianism and egalitarianism, fail on this count. They propose a task for the state, such as the maximization of preference-satisfaction or overall equality, but they say very little about what form the state is allowed to take in pursuit of that task, perhaps because the form of the state has little apparent bearing on the extent to which utility or equality is realized. This failure must have a chilling effect on any reflective imagination, certainly on the imagination of those who are actively engaged with politics. For who is to assume control of the apparatus whereby the high ideal proposed is to be targeted and promoted? And what is to guard against that apparatus assuming gargantuan proportions, as it claims resources adequate to the dimensions of the brief with which it is charged?

But it is not only high ideals like utility and equality that are in danger of failing this first desideratum. Even a comparatively low, apparently modest, ideal like freedom as noninterference also does badly. It requires that the state practice only forms of interference that make for a decrease in interference overall. But that is consistent with the best form of state—the state that does best in promoting overall noninterference—being a benevolent despotism, as adherents of the ideal have always allowed (Paley 1825, 166; Berlin 1958). The ideal is not suitably broad, then; it says little or nothing of significance about the constitutional form that the state should take. Unlike the ideal of freedom as nondomination, for example, it does not provide a basis on which to argue for the attractions of democracy.

A DEEP IDEAL

A political ideal is deep as distinct from broad when the policies it looks likely to support cover the bulk of the complaints that people might want the state to address. Any ideal is designed to answer to a complaint, as the ideal of freedom as nondomination answers to the domination complaint: the complaint of being stood over by others and subjected to their will. The depth desideratum is that satisfaction of the complaint to which an ideal answers should be likely to ensure that a variety of other politically plausible complaints are satisfied too.

For us the most obvious example of an ideal that fails in depth is that of freedom as noninterference, since this ideal might be satisfied fully in the presence of appalling poverty or exposure to noninterfering forms of control.[6] But another salient example is provided by the ideal of equality. To invoke the well-known leveling-down objection to that ideal (Parfit 2000), the best way of securing equality may be to reduce everyone to a state of relative penury. If the inequality complaint were satisfied in that way, then its satisfaction would not entail the satisfaction of even the complaint that is associated most strongly with it: the complaint against poverty and the lack of resources that it involves. On the contrary, the satisfaction of the inequality complaint might increase the ground for complaints about poverty, not remove them.

A ROBUST IDEAL

Apart from being broad and deep, an energizing political ideal ought also to provide a robust basis for ordering the different ways things may be. Thus the ideal ought to be capable, at least in principle, of providing advice on what the state should do, no matter how imperfect the point at which it is located and no matter how partial the various improvements possible at that point. The requirement, in other words, is that the ideal provide a metric that allows us in principle to determine which of a number of imperfect realizations of the ideal is actually better. Unless a political philosophy satisfies this requirement, it will be incapable of providing guidance on real-world problems.[7]

An approach that will fail this requirement is what John Rawls (1971) describes as ideal theory. An ideal theory is designed to tell us what is just, or what is in other ways desirable, under certain idealizing assumptions (O'Neill 1987). Rawls's own early theory of justice made two idealizing assumptions: first, that people in the just society will give the theory credence and, second, that they will comply in general with the theory (Rawls 1971). While softening the credence assumption, Rawls stuck by the assumption of general compliance in his later work on political liberalism (Rawls 1993). He departed most thoroughly from ideal theory only in his last work on the law of peoples (Rawls 1999).

The ideal-theory approach necessarily makes a political ideal incapable of providing a complete or robust basis for ordering available alternatives. It means that we are given information on what makes for satisfaction of the ideal only under the assumption that the philosophy commands general compliance and perhaps general credence. Faced with two scenarios in which compliance is only partial, we will not be provided with a criterion by which to rank them against one another. If one of the scenarios is the status quo, and the other a scenario that political policy could be used to realize, we will be left unguided as to whether to introduce that policy or not. An ideal of this partial character might provide us with images of inaccessible perfection—and we do not deny that that may be a worthwhile accomplishment—but it will not be capable of energizing us in day-to-day politics.

An ideal may fail to be energizing, however, on two further grounds, unrelated to breadth or depth or robustness. The first is that as an ideal it may be excessively intrusive, the second that it may be excessively austere.

A NONINTRUSIVE IDEAL

An ideal for state action will be excessively intrusive if it is the sort of ideal that ought to be left to the initiative and effort of individual human beings, not put in political hands. Many who embrace the ideal of freedom as nondomination will think of individual autonomy—the self-mastery that any individual might hope to achieve—as a further, richer ideal. But it would be a mistake, in the republican view, to think of such autonomy as a political ideal rather than as an ideal that should be left to individuals to pursue (or fail to pursue) in their own way. Let a coercive state assume the task of promoting such autonomy and it will have grounds to assert itself in people's lives on issues of how they are raised, what they read, and who they associate with. Without endorsing his version of freedom as noninterference, we sympathize with Isaiah Berlin's (1958) attack on the chilling specter of such an invasive state. The ideal that would support that state may warm up the less reflective, even inflame them, but it cannot be expected to serve as a robustly energizing target.

A NONAUSTERE IDEAL

The final way in which a political ideal may fail is the complement of this last mode of failure. The ideal may be too austere to serve as an attractive goal, failing to connect with the concerns and complaints of ordinary people, or connecting only partially with them. We see a failure of this kind in various ideals that enjoy a prominence in academic and bureaucratic circles. Consider the ideal of equality, for example, or the ideal of utility. Each has a certain logic attached to it but neither connects, in our view, with concerns that people routinely feel and avow. They connect, at best, with only a subset of such concerns.

What avowed complaint is meant to be satisfied by the call on the state to promote material equality for its own sake: this, as distinct from a call on the state to promote material equality as a means to equal legal status, or as a prerequisite to a sufficiency in material goods, or whatever? We suspect that full equality, presented as something intrinsically desirable, is an aesthetic ideal that has a certain attraction for theorists, not an ideal that answers to any routinely avowed complaint. At most it answers to complaints of envy that few will stand behind and avow.[8]

What is true of equality is true also of utility. People may complain in politics about not having access to this or that resource or opportunity, and the lack of such access may impact on their levels of happiness. But people are not generally disposed to make a complaint to others, let alone a complaint that is supposed to engage the state, about their lack of happiness. It may be a beguiling aesthetic ideal, a design specification for the engineering of society, that people should enjoy a maximum of the happiness available to them. But it does not have the makings of a political ideal that can engage hearts as well as minds.

To cast such a cold eye on political ideals of equality and utility is not to say that the efforts of economists and other social scientists to provide measures of equality and utility are unimportant. The audits in which societies are compared in this way may be of great importance in indicating that things are going relatively well or badly in a given society and they may prompt an extra degree of interrogation of government. But the terms in which questions are put to the government will have to engage distinct ideals—ideals with a hold on people's hearts—if they are to facilitate political engagement as distinct from strategic or bureaucratic planning.

The Energizing Republican Ideal

As the republican ideal of freedom as nondomination proves to be a shareable and realistic ideal in politics, it also does extremely well against the desiderata associated with this final condition. It is broad, it is deep, it is robust. And while it is not so rich as to intrude on personal life, it is not so austere that it fails to engage with ordinary human complaints.

The breadth of the ideal has already been addressed in other chapters. The republican ideal requires government to pursue policies for the reduction of domination over its citizens by private parties and groups, domestic and international. But it requires at the same time that the government that protects against private domination in that way should not itself be a source of public domination. It should not perpetrate the very domination against which it seeks to protect its citizens. This requirement has deep and demanding implications for the organization of the state. As we have seen, it argues that the state should pursue its business according to a discipline of general, promulgated law, under a separation that authorizes distinct centers of power, and within a culture of democratic transparency that exposes government to constant invigilation and routine contestation. It bears as much on how government is conducted as on what government seeks to achieve.

The republican ideal is deep as well as broad, as becomes obvious in light of the very different deficits that can trigger the domination complaint (Pettit 2005). Let the infrastructure of law or economy, environment or education, fail and there will be a widespread exposure to domination on the part of those who are weaker and exposed. Let the vulnerable in domestic, workplace, or cultural contexts not enjoy adequate rights or powers or options compared to others, and they will suffer domination in those relationships. Let domestic crime or international political or commercial bullying threaten a population, and the victims will find themselves subject to dominating invigilation, intimidation, and even outright forms of uncontrolled interference. Let some domestic individuals or bodies—say, corporations or churches—grow in power within a society and, without any independent change in their circumstances, others will find themselves relatively disempowered and dominated. Because of the myriad ways in which domination can occur, the rectification of the domination complaint will ensure the satisfaction of many more specific complaints as well. If the state combats domination, then it will have to combat the anarchy, ignorance, and poverty, and the bullying, coercion, and violence, which figure across the range of complaints that people routinely make against government.

In addition to these virtues, freedom as nondomination also represents a robust ideal. It is defined in such a way that there is never any block in principle to determining what it requires by way of ameliorating any situation, even when the situation is highly imperfect and the improvements available are only partial. There may be a difficulty, of course, in determining that a particular change will make for an improvement, as distinct from being no better or no worse than the status quo. But that may be a product of an unavoidable vagueness and need not be a cause of regret. The important point is that the republican ideal will be defined for an open-ended range of contexts, not just for contexts that meet certain idealizing assumptions such as the assumption of general compliance. In any context the ideal will argue for that improvement, assuming there is one available, that makes for a higher degree of nondomination overall.

Turning to the last two desiderata of an energizing ideal, it should be equally clear that the ideal of freedom as nondomination is neither excessively intrusive nor excessively austere. What it hails is a condition that the coercive state is uniquely well positioned to help to secure: a condition in which people enjoy such rights, powers, and options that they can command an equal status with others. In charging the state with promoting the enjoyment of that condition, republican theory does not reach into domains of personal life where, intuitively, we would not want it to play a part. The ideal of nondomination may appeal on the grounds that, if only people are protected in this way, then they may hope to achieve the autonomy—the positive, personal freedom—that consists in organizing their lives according to their reflectively endorsed values. But republican theory does not give the state any responsibility for promoting personal autonomy as such. It is a theory of the *res publica*, the business of the public. Thus the state's authority ceases at a boundary where most of us would want it to cease; it is not allowed to encroach on what most of us see as the domain of the soul.

But if it is not too intrusive, neither is the ideal of nondomination too austere. On the contrary, it connects with a concern, endemic in our social species, for enjoying standing, and commanding respect, in the eyes of our fellows. Who is not moved by the thought of being able to walk tall, as someone who is fully incorporated into a matrix of effective social and political protection? Who is not attracted in particular by the prospect of being able to do this as a matter of general, community consciousness? And who is not going to be impressed, given even the weakest sense of social solidarity, by the ideal of a society in which everyone can live in that same security and that same consciousness of security?

The ideal of nondomination may not connect with all the concerns that people have in their private lives, espousing a nonintrusive profile, but it does engage with a full range of concerns in their public relations with one another. We drew attention earlier

to the wealth of terms for describing the destitution of the dominated, and we sketched the associated picture of what freedom can
achieve as it enables people to walk tall and look others in the eye.
This ideal can hardly fail to touch the personal and moral imagination and to engage people's feelings and desires. Not to care about
freedom as nondomination would be not to care about life itself,
or at least not about the only life available to us, which is life in
the society of our fellows.

Conclusion

We have seen that if a political philosophy is to serve its proper
role in public life there are three broad conditions that the ideal it
recommends should fulfill. The ideal should be shareable, realistic,
and energizing. It should be capable of commanding allegiance on
all sides of even a pluralistic society; it should presuppose only
such resources of motivation and cognition as are likely to be
available, or capable of being made available, in social life; and
it should have the ability to capture and energize the minds and
hearts of ordinary people.

The various distinctions that we have drawn in this discussion
are caught in the accompanying diagram (page 160), which may
be helpful in summarizing the demands on political ideals that are
fit to serve in public life.

These are big demands to place on any ideal or set of ideals
and, as we have tried to indicate, they are demands that many of
our political philosophies fail to meet: many but not all. Our un-
apologetically partisan argument has been that here as elsewhere
the civic republican philosophy of government does particularly
well. The ideal of freedom as nondomination is perfectly shareable, having nothing sectional or sectarian about it. It is a realistic
ideal to the extent that it does not make extravagant assumptions
about the motivational or cognitive capacities of human beings:
and it holds out an energizing goal. It is broad enough to impose
constitutional constraints on the state, deep enough to support a
demanding set of political policies, and robust enough to have les-

Political ideals should be

I. Shareable { non-sectional, conceptually and contingently, and
               non-sectarian, conceptually and contingently

II. Realistic { in its motivational assumptions, and
                in its cognitive assumptions

III. Energizing, i.e. { broad,
                        deep,
                        robust,
                        non-intrusive, and
                        non-austere

sons to teach at any point on the spectrum of political imperfection. Most important of all, it reaches deep into the wellspring of human concerns without ceasing to be a political ideal that can safely be committed to the charge of a coercive state.

Civic republicanism is not a fixed ideology and it does not offer a blueprint for the ideal state or the ideal international order. On the contrary, its normative and institutional implications for contemporary polities, in the many cultural variations they assume, remain to be fully elaborated and tested. But one of its signal virtues, as we have sought to establish in this chapter, is that it is at least available for practical testing. Unlike more idealized competitors, it is a research program that can be explored, not just by thinking out its implications in theory, but also by putting them into political practice (Lovett and Pettit 2009). It is available for use in the public square as well as in the academic seminar.

NOTES

CHAPTER 1
THE SPANISH CONTEXT

1. I am indebted to many colleagues and friends who have read initial versions of this chapter. I thank especially William Chislett, Robert Fishman, Carles Boix, Félix Ovejero, Roberto Gargarella, and Águeda Quiroga for their useful comments and suggestions—and sometimes criticisms, equally useful—that prevented me of making many mistakes. An earlier version of the chapter was also presented at the Iberian Study Group, at the Minda de Gunzburg Center for European Studies at Harvard University. I am particularly grateful to Sebastián Royo and Sofía Pérez for having invited me to the Center and for their valuable suggestions. As pointed out in the Preface, the University Center for Human Values at Princeton University offered me the opportunity and a dream environment at an appropriate distance from my country to discuss my opinions with Philip and to write this chapter and my contribution to other chapters in this book. I want to thank, finally, Julie Scales who took care of the text from the stylistic point of view and corrected many infelicitous expressions in my imperfect English.

2. An initial terminological caveat is appropriate. There are, in my view, good reasons for using the word "president" to translate the Spanish "*presidente*," applied to the head of the government as established in the Spanish Constitution of 1978, instead of "prime minister." The exact technical expression is *presidente del gobierno* (president of the government). Even though Spain's form of government is a monarchy and not a republic, and the monarch is considered the head of the state, he holds purely symbolic powers, and the president of the government is, in almost all effects, the one who governs the country. The president of the government is certainly the head of the ministers who form the government, but he is actually not a minister himself. Thus it seems inappropriate to call him prime minister, as is usual in English. In any case, in order to avoid confusion, we have decided to use that term here.

3. For systematic coverage of many aspects of Spain in English, see the monthly review by William Chislett (2004–9. For a recent and rigorous introduction to Spanish politics, see Gunther and Montero (2009).

4. The terms "liberal" and "liberalism" mean something quite different in the United States and in Europe, as in the academic sphere. In Europe, they refer basically to an economic position, and are associated with the right-wing tradition

in support of free markets and deregulation, while in the United States "liberal" is usually applied to a left-wing political viewpoint basically concerning social issues, as opposed to conservative. The latter is indeed much closer to the very origins of the word in Spain at the beginning of the nineteenth century. The scholarly meaning associated with the word "liberalism." in both Europe and United States, even though imprecise, captures part of both sensibilities. The ambiguity in the term can be removed by differentiating, first, between political and economic liberalism, the latter being much closer to the American understanding; and then, more importantly, between right-wing liberalism or libertarianism (or neoliberalism), and left-wing liberalism or liberal egalitarianism (see chapter 2 for treatment of this topic).

5. Spain's first democratic elections after Francisco Franco's long dictatorship came in 1977 (Franco died in 1975) and the current constitution was enacted in 1978. From that time until the present, Spain has had only five prime ministers, three of them coming from the center or the center-right (Adolfo Suárez, 1976–81, Leopoldo Calvo Sotelo, 1981–82, and José María Aznar, 1996–2004) and two from the center-left (González, 1982–96, and Rodríguez Zapatero, from 2004 until presumably 2012). For some accounts in English of the transition to democracy in Spain, see Gunther and Montero (2009, chap. 1), Maravall (1982), and Pérez Díaz (1993).

6. The PSOE is a long-standing political party in Spain, founded in 1879 by Pablo Iglesias, and was very active during both the Spanish Second Republic (1931–39) and the Civil War (1936–39). The party was banned by Franco in 1936, and legalized again in 1977, at which time it officially endorsed a Marxist ideology. In 1982, the PSOE obtained a huge congressional majority over its main competitor, the center-right Unión de Centro Democrático (UCD) or Democratic Center Union (a coalition party which has since disappeared), and González was elected as prime minister. It was the first time that a clear opponent to Franco was elected to lead the country. For an account of the main parties in Spain and their role in recent democratic politics, see Gunther and Montero (2009, chap. 4).

7. Felipe González had been elected secretary general of the party in 1974, in the clandestine 26th party conference held in Suresnes, a suburb of Paris (France). It took him five years to persuade his political colleagues to transform the party into a standard social-democratic one, similar to its counterparts in the rest of Western Europe, thus abandoning Marxism.

8. The Spanish constitution does not place a limit on terms, and therefore allows a prime minister to be reelected an indefinite number of times. This is not to be seen as a danger of authoritarianism, since the Spanish political system is a parliamentary system, not a presidential one. The prime minister is elected by the Congress of Deputies (the Spanish "lower house," equivalent to the U.S. House of Representatives), not directly by the people; and his term can be ended by congress itself through a *moción de censura*, a constructive vote of no confidence. A parliamentary (absolute) majority, then, can censure or curtail the tenure of

the prime minister as soon as it loses confidence in him (the Spanish Constitution distinguishes between an "absolute majority," more than 50% of deputies, a minimum of 176 out of the 350 deputies, and equivalent to just a "majority" in the United States, and a "simple majority," more votes in favor than against, and equivalent to "plurality"). On the other hand, the prime minister has no veto power regarding laws passed by the congress. This renders the prime minister much less powerful than a president in a presidential system, and much more dependent on the parliament, especially on the congress. For an overview of the constitutional framework of the Spanish democracy, see Gunther and Montero (2009, chap. 2).

9. The Spanish welfare state included the three traditional pillars of the European welfare state model: universal and public education, a universal and public health system, and a massive social security system with generalized pensions for workers' retirement and subsidies for unemployed workers. According to an extended understanding, the Spanish model differed from those of the central and northern European countries in the degree of protection and implementation of each of these pillars, as well as in the size of the public employment sector (Esping-Andersen 1990). For an analysis of the PSOE performance and its social democratic project, see Boix (1998).

10. Euskadi Ta Askatasuna (ETA), that is, "Basque Homeland and Freedom," is a terrorist band created in the Basque Country in 1969 to resist Franco, officially espousing a far-left ideology and having radical nationalist separatist propensities. After Franco's death, it prolonged its activity with the aim of achieving the independence of the Basque Country, although part of the group dropped their arms and became a democratic political party. ETA has killed more than 800 people in Spain in the last four decades, including soldiers, politicians, and police officers, as well as civilians. It has obviously represented one of the major political and social problems in democratic Spain.

11. The PP was founded in 1976 as Alianza Popular (Popular Alliance), by Manuel Fraga, a former Minister of Tourism under Franco, and refounded by Fraga himself in 1989 as Partido Popular. It was born as a conservative party, but it later integrated the Christian Democrats and liberal sensibilities in Spain under a common center-right umbrella. José María Aznar was a strong leader in the party from 1989 until 2004, transforming it into a cohesive and modern political force, functionally and hierarchically organized, and leading it to a deep ideological renewal abandoning any Francoist or undemocratic vestiges. See Gunther and Montero (2009, 130–32).

12. Spain has a multiparty system, but its peculiar electoral regulation favors concentration in the hands of the two larger parties, namely, the PSOE and the Partido Popular (PP). The features that distinguish that system are fifty-two small electoral districts; a nonproportional distribution of deputies (the less crowded districts are overrepresented); and a minimum-vote threshold, with a d'Hondt formula used to allocate seats among parties within each district, Although the

third national party in number of votes, the Communist Party or its successor co-alition Izquierda Unida (IU), obtained 4% of votes in 1977 and more than 10% in 1996, it has always been underrepresented in the Spanish Congress; it is now the sixth party in congress by number of deputies, holding only two seats. The two main nationalist parties in Spain are the Partido Nacionalista Vasco (PNV) in the Basque Country, and Convergencia i Unió—Convergence and Unity—(CIU), in Catalonia, two historically rich areas of Spain. Despite their small parliamentary representation, they are often necessary when the two larger parties fail to reach an (absolute) majority on their own. The strength of a prime minister in Spain depends largely on the ability to gain a sufficient supportive majority in parliament. First, as mentioned above, (s)he can be terminated by a majority of the congress through a vote of no confidence. And, second, although the government, as well as the political parties represented in congress, can submit legal initiatives for parliamentary approval, it requires a sufficient majority or plurality both in the Congress of Deputies and in the Senate to pass the law (the Senate, the "upper house," has the power to reject or amend a bill passed by the Congress of Deputies. However, in both cases the Congress can vote on a bill for a second time, thereby overriding the Senate). Then the distribution of seats in both houses of parliament—taking place simultaneously after each election, in principle, every four years—is crucial because it determines the spirit and the content of each parliamentary session. If the winning party does not obtain an (absolute) majority (that is, as explained above, more than 50% of seats in congress), which happened twice under González (1982 and 1986) and once under Aznar (2000), it is required to negotiate with other minor parties for general support over the term of parliament. This support is necessary to support the election of the prime minister, to approve the annual budgets, and finally to prevent the censure or vote of no confidence in the prime minister. Minor parties will normally use the fact that their support is required to bargain about individual laws to be passed. See Gunther and Montero (2009, chaps. 2–4).

13. FAES, the acronym for Fundación para el Análisis y los Estudios Sociales (Foundation for Analysis and Social Studies), was established in 2002, gathering under its umbrella all the previous smaller foundations on the Spanish Right. Modeled explicitly after conservative American think tanks like the Heritage Foundation or the American Enterprise Institute, it has played an unprecedented leading role in the modernization and consolidation of the Right's ideas in Spain.

14. The two leaders, together with British Prime Minister Tony Blair and Italian Prime Minister Silvio Berlusconi, formed an international alliance that supported the invasion of Iraq. This was announced at the meeting held on the Azores Islands on March 16, 2003 which was attended by all but Berlusconi.

15. After the González defeat in 1996, and for the first time in its history, the party used a primary election process for nominating its candidate for the next legislative election. The winner was José Borrell, who was preferred by most of the party's militants, but lacked nevertheless the support of his own party's

ruling structures, the so-called *aparato*. After a corruption scandal that touched him indirectly, he was obliged to resign his candidacy in 1999, thereby making José Almunia—his opponent in the primary election—the final candidate. For a brief account of the PSOE's leadership struggles, see Gunther and Montero (2009, 126).

16. The most important of such divisions separated the old-fashioned *aparato* from the large base of party militants. But there were also tensions between some competing territorial units, as well as between several ideological trends and factions. The PSOE is a federation of smaller parties territorially based in the Autonomous Communities, some of which are very influential in the party's structure at the national level, as is the Andalusian one. The Autonomous Communities (Comunidades Autónomas) are the regions into which the country is politically and administratively divided, and enjoy a high level of political decentralization, comparable in some respects to a federal structure, although lower in others.

17. José Bono had been president of the Autonomous Community of Castilla–La Mancha since 1983. Matilde Fernández had been Minister of Social Affairs under González and was supported by the Alfonso Guerra sector, a former deputy prime minister with González, and then a rival in the party. Nueva Vía was formed by people such as José Blanco, Jesús Caldera, Carme Chacón, José Andrés Torres Mora, and Juan Fernando López Aguilar, most of whom would be later Ministers with Zapatero. For a brief description of the rise of Nueva Vía and the victory of Zapatero as a secretary general in that conference, see Papell (2008, 21–31) and Campillo (2004, chaps. 10 and 11). Personal testimonies of Zapatero and other members of Nueva Vía are collected in de Toro (2007, 46–109).

18. The clear hands-down favorite was Bono. He was publicly endorsed by González and by most of the party leaders, but Fernández had a chance at winning too, as she was supported by a small but powerful minority group. Zapatero won with a slight margin, obtaining 414 votes (41.69%), while Bono got 405 (40.79%), Fernández 109 (10.98%), and Díez 65 (6.55%). According to some participants in that event, it was his hopeful rhetoric proposing a deep change that persuaded the majority of electors to elect him. Part of the explanation also had to do with the bad electoral strategy followed by the *aparato* in support of its candidate José Bono. They strongly pressed the militants to gain their votes, which turned out to be counterproductive. The reason the militants voted for Zapatero, and not for any of the other, much better-known candidates, seems to be that he had a discourse based on proposing deep but hopeful changes, in contrast to the agonistic claims made by others (Campillo 2004, 272–77; Papell 2008, 27). According to María Teresa Fernández de la Vega—the would-be deputy prime minister in the Spanish government under Zapatero, but not yet a member of Nueva Vía— "what he offered us was collective self-esteem" (de Toro 2007, 59).

19. "We have an unequivocal project for this country; we have planted seeds in this conference; we are the seeds to be grown, in order to gather up all the citizenry to work for a new and distinct Spain." This and the following excerpts are

extracted from the text of his speech, which can be found on the PSOE website (Rodríguez Zapatero 2000).

20. Emphasis added. This message was a complete break from previous party discourse, especially considering the enormous influence González exerted in the party and the nostalgia of many socialists for his four terms in the government.

21. In part because of the enduring influence of González mentioned above. Zapatero himself admired him and was captivated by his charisma. Indeed, he decided to join the PSOE after listening to González at a rally in 1979 (Campillo 2004, chap. 1).

22. As expressed in the interview included in chapter 4, Zapatero affirms that "in effect, freedom is the essential element. I have always thought, since I was young, that personal freedom is the essential value of politics" (see chapter 4).

23. "We all will work with dignity, with capacity for dialogue, with tolerance, with that form, that style which must permanently distinguish those who feel and think as socialists; a style of conviction, a style of respect, a style of work, of work well-done" (Rodríguez Zapatero 2000).

24. As his concluding remarks show: "this will be the way to be respected and to obtain once again the support of the majority [of voters]. I have no doubt about it. This is a fascinating task. I invite you to develop a new hope" (Rodríguez Zapatero 2000). Words like "thrill," "optimism," "future," "opportunity," "success," and "victory" were repeated again and again throughout the speech.

25. It is not, of course, that social democracy had been endorsing or even approving the kind of Marxist-Leninist communist ideology supposedly represented by the Soviet Union (although this was, for historic reasons, the case of the PSOE prior to 1979). Rather, a particular and traditional feature of European social democracy had been its opposition to communism on the Left. They demonstrated their ideals by endorsing democracy, by pursuing the protection of workers' interests within a framework of rights and liberties, and by choosing only legal methods for achieving these goals. Thus, for quite some time there was a sharp contrast between social democratic and communist parties both in the kind of goals adopted and in the means selected to achieve them. However, social democracy had always taken advantage of the existence and influence of the extremist ideology of the Left to present itself as moderate, centrist, and sensitive to doctrine. As has been stated, the fear of communism explains the widespread acceptance of social democracy for most of the second half of the twentieth century (see Schumpeter 1942).

26. This was satirized by the Left in all Europe under the French label of *pensée unique* (unique thinking), an expression which was also very successful in Spain and Latin America with the translation *pensamiento único*.

27. Jean Chrétien and Wim Kok were elected prime ministers of Canada and the Netherlands in 1993 and 1994, respectively. Australia had a social democratic government from 1983 to 1996 and there were social democratic governments in Latin America as well.

28. For the situation in the United Kingdom, for instance, see Crick (1997, p. 344–51) and Tonkin (1998). New Labour's first attempt in the early 1990s at endorsing a public philosophy was to adopt some values and proposals from communitarianism, like the idea of a "stakeholder society" proposed by Hutton, Etzioni, and others (Temple 2000, 303–4).

29. It was addressed to the progressive center-left in Britain and elsewhere, and intended to achieve "a just society which maximizes the freedom and potential of all our people—equal worth, opportunity for all, responsibility and community" (Blair 1998), quoted by Temple (2000, 308).

30. As pointed out by Temple, "Despite their commitment to social democracy, experimentation rather than adherence to some rigid ideological framework is (allegedly) the guiding characteristic of Giddens' and Blair's Third Way" (Temple 2000, 312).

31. In part because of this mildness in differentiating itself from Thatcher's neoliberalism, the Third Way was rejected or poorly welcomed by other European social democrats. Regarding this doctrine, Jospin declared: "if the Third Way lies between ultraliberalism and state socialism I'm interested. If the Third Way locates itself between (neo)liberalism and social democracy, count me out," quoted by Temple (2000, 313). Without relying on a particular doctrine, or at least without identifying with a particular label, the French social-democratic party was trying to renew the Left. Its most well-known initiative was the 35-hour work week, which was introduced by the Martine Aubry Law in February 2000 (the previous general limit was 39 hours a week). But the complete set of measures proposed by Jospin was not enthusiastically accepted and the party suffered a severe defeat in the following legislative election in 2002. The case of Gerhard Schroeder in Germany is more complicated. His personal proposal was the idea of a *Neue Mitte* (a "new center"), following intuitions similar to those of the Third Way: he attempted to capture the electoral center by making some concessions to the Right and to neoliberalism. But his proposal was at least as abstract and ambiguous as the Third Way, and much less influential.

32. For an example of the general perception among Leftist intellectuals in Spain about the Third Way, see Vallespín (2000b); and regarding the need for a more solid political philosophy, see Vallespín (2000a).

33. Another important reason for rejecting the Third Way was that, as pointed out above, Tony Blair was one of José María Aznar's principal international allies. Their alliance was never based on shared political values, but nevertheless it was uneasy for Zapatero to approach Blair's doctrine under such circumstances.

34. There is a cultural difference between English speakers and Spanish speakers in understanding the term "pragmatic." In Anglo-Saxon countries, pragmatism generally is considered a positive feature of politicians and political leaders. Pragmatism means efficiency and nondogmatism about the means for achieving the same goals. In continental Europe, pragmatism has this meaning as well, but the most prominent one is instead associated with cynicism and skepticism about

principles; to be pragmatic is to justify any means in order to obtain the desired outcomes. This different understanding may explain part of the Spanish skepticism about the Third Way. Pragmatism, when applied to a political leader, is not actually a complimentary term, at least on the Left. It is nothing to be proud of. But this is not the whole story. The interesting issue with the Third Way is that, as pointed out above, it can be regarded as pragmatic under the continental view as well, and this was disappointing for Nueva Vía, which according to Torres Mora, one of its members, was avid about stronger principles (Torres Mora 2008).

35. As pointed out above, "liberal" means something different in the European context, where a liberal is basically a right-wing advocate of free markets and deregulation, than in the United States, which makes this statement unfortunate. See note 4 for further discussion of the distinction.

36. Traditionally the word was used to refer to anarchist positions and was very important during the Spanish Second Republic (1931–39) and the Civil War (1936–39). This is actually the most common meaning in the Spanish political tradition. The other meaning, imported by the academic spheres, is the translation of the English word "libertarian," which usually refers to the far Right, neo-liberal conception of politics and justice, though many scholars and translators opt for "libertariano," precisely to avoid confusion with the first meaning.

37. Pettit's republicanism, to be sure, was not the only contemporary political theory that Zapatero and other Nueva Vía members explored and found congenial. John Rawls's liberal egalitarianism and Jürgen Habermas's deliberative democratic theory were also regarded as inspiring for their task. Zapatero considered Rawls a positive influence for the 1980s Spanish socialism, but he was looking for something new and different, and Pettit's theory was viewed as particularly powerful and useful for his purposes (see the interview included in chapter 4). Rawls and Habermas were, however, the preferred source of inspiration for a minority within Nueva Vía, represented by the would-be Minister Jordi Sevilla (2002). For a review of Zapatero's collaborators who were nourishing the party with new doctrine at that time, see Sánchez (2002) and García Agustín (2006).

38. To accentuate this distance from the Third Way, Zapatero later refused to attend an international meeting of social democratic leaders dealing with the renovation of the Left, which was held in London in the summer of 2003. This meeting, hosted by Tony Blair, included all the top figures of the Left in the world: Bill Clinton (United States), Gerhard Schroeder (Germany), Lionel Jospin (France), Wim Kok (Netherland), Jean Chrétien (Canada), and Massimo D'Alema (Italy), in addition to certain presidents of South American countries such as Argentina, Chile, and Brazil. But only a week after this meeting, he participated in an academic seminar in Madrid with distinguished political philosophers like Benjamin Barber, Zygmunt Bauman, Alessandro Ferrara, Fernando Vallespín, Fernando Savater, and Félix Ovejero, to assess possible paths for the renovation of the Spanish Left, paying particular attention to republicanism; Pettit had been invited but had a prior commitment. Zapatero was launching a message: he shared the desire to

renovate and modernize the Left with his international colleagues, but considered the Third Way inadequate for that purpose, at least in Spain (Barbería 2004; García Agustín 2006).

39. See also his explanation of the connection between freedom and democracy in the interview included in chapter 4.

40. This new style, in particular when contrasted with Aznar's tough one, made him appear to some analysts and colleagues to be too soft, and perhaps too naive. For this reason he earned the nickname of Bambi, alluding to the deer in the animated Disney film.

41. One of the requirements of the parliamentary system in Spain is that the prime minister must appear and defend his policies in congress at least once a year. This debate on the state of the nation starts with the prime minister's annual address summarizing his initiatives in the last year. This is followed by the criticisms or questions raised by the speakers of all parliamentary forces and the prime minister's subsequent response. The whole process takes place over the course of at least two long days. It is one of the major political events every year concerning the relations between the executive and the legislature.

42. For an introduction to the phenomenon of demonstrations in Spain in general, see Fishman (2007b).

43. When Aznar first ran against González, he committed himself to be in office for only two terms, and, once his terms had ended, he personally nominated Rajoy as his successor. On the other hand, the difference in polls between Rajoy and Zapatero had been constantly decreasing throughout the whole campaign, and was tiny at the very end.

44. Although the PP has always rejected this charge, the Spanish Supreme Court, when sentencing the terrorists arrested for that crime, found no evidence of the ETA's "crazy hypothesis" and ruled that the government was at the very least negligent in their use of information (Tribunal Supremo 2007).

45. The PP held that this popular reaction was promoted by the PSOE in order to generate a perception of manipulation by the government only a few hours before the election. But even if this were true of the small public demonstrations held in front of the PP's offices, there certainly was a more general perception that the government's statements were obscure and unfair.

46. No doubt part of the reason for this shift was that, as pointed out above, Spanish people were mostly opposed to Spain's participation in the Iraq War, and they blamed Aznar for having decided on that participation. The shift came not only because some people who were previously going to vote for the PP shifted their vote to support the PSOE, but mainly because there were many people who were not initially going to vote who decided to cast their ballots against the PP. This seems supported by the voter turn-out in the election, which rose to 77%, while it had only been 69% in the 2000 general election. Surely some of those who shifted the vote, or who decided to go out to vote just after the attack, were motivated because they blamed the PP for having involved Spain in the war. But

most of them were probably motivated by a negative assessment of the government's management of the crisis. For a rigorous and illuminating account of the turn in the elections, as an application of Weberian methodology, see Fishman (2007a, 261–89).

47. Since Spain has a parliamentary system, the prime minister is elected not directly by the people, but by the congress in a nomination process or investiture once it has been constituted according to the results in the general elections. This is the second task of the new congress, just after electing a president of the chamber (the equivalent of the U.S. Speaker of the House), and his vice-presidents and secretaries.

48. The nomination process in the congress is called *investidura* (investiture), and the candidate to prime minister, who must already be deputy of the chamber, is required to defend his program for the government in advance in order to convince the other deputies of its appropriateness. This defense, which includes a question and answer process with the speakers of the main parties represented, is called the *discurso de investidura* (the investiture or nomination speech). This process takes usually several exhausting days of debate before voting. To be elected prime minister, a candidate must be voted for by an (absolute) majority of the chamber on the first round of votes, or by a plurality on a second round (more votes in favor than against).

49. This may well be inspired by the idea of a decent society, as articulated by the philosopher Avishai Margalit (1996).

50. It also included the goals of advancing the process for territorial decentralization of the Autonomous Communities, reforming the organization of the Congress and Senate, modernizing the judiciary, providing security and beginning a process of constitutional amendments—which was finally blocked by the PP.

51. In his response to Rodríguez Sánchez, speaker of the Mixed Group and the Bloque Nacionalista Galego, he specified: "I want a society politically united that uses critical judgment to its maximum capacity; I want an active citizenry, and to have this critical and interested citizenry, pluralism needs to be present; deliberation, in which the problems and interests of all citizens must be represented, needs to be the constant" (Rodríguez Zapatero 2004d, 110). Finally, in response to Barkos Berruezo, speaker of Nafarroa Bai (a nationalist coalition in Navarra), he explicitly stated: "We want to make a civic democracy. We want to make a democracy of citizens, of people who are and feel like citizens every day. We want to make a positive, active, and participatory democracy, and this is a demanding ideal for the citizenry. It is demanding not only for the government, but also a requirement for the citizenry, for it to take its responsibility when government, when politics, opens its doors" (Rodríguez Zapatero 2004d, 121).

52. Emphasis added. In response to Rodríguez Sánchez, speaker of Bloque Nacionalista Galego (the Galician Nationalist Party), referring to the social phenomenon of the violence against women, Zapatero stated: "It is the wicked by-product of several successive cultural models and values that we have been

historically dragging along, a product that can be translated into one idea: domi-nation. You will remember that at the end of my speech yesterday I declared that my government will fight against any form of arbitrary domination. To keep all people from being dominated is to secure freedom, and of course my government will be militant against any form of domination, of abuse" (Rodríguez Zapatero 2004d, 109).

53. In effect, Bush never forgave Zapatero for pulling out. Zapatero is actu-ally one of the few European leaders never to have been officially invited to the White House during the Bush Administration. Zapatero saw this decision, in any case, as fulfilling one of his main electoral promises. As he declared to the French newspaper *Le Monde* a few months later, "my first decision ... was not applauded by the American administration. But it will get better. The country of Jefferson can understand what a democratic decision means and what a commitment to citizens is" (Rodríguez Zapatero 2004a).

54. During his days in Spain in 2004, Pettit lectured in Madrid and Barcelona, and was interviewed by the most prestigious newspapers, including *El País* (Martí Font 2004), *La Vanguardia* (Gamper 2004), and *El Periódico*. He was also inter-viewed on television, in the most popular political program on the Catalan public channel TV3 at that time, "La Nit al Dia." Later in October, after a series of lec-tures in several towns in Catalonia he was interviewed in *El Periódico* (Navarro 2004), and other smaller Catalan newspapers, like *El Punt*, *Diari de Girona*, *Diari de Tarragona*, *Segre*, and *La Mañana*. The ultimate goal of all these public appearances was to explain to Spanish people the content and appeal of his po-litical philosophy, the philosophy endorsed by the government.

55. It is not true, as some Spanish journalists have maintained, that Pettit had special access to Zapatero at that time or afterward. He never privately advised the prime minister, and he certainly did not take part in any of the government's ordinary decision-making. Besides three interviews with Zapatero in 2004, 2006, and 2007 (they were private but covered intensely by the media), the way in which Pettit inspired Zapatero's government was mainly through his books, lec-tures, and interviews with the press.

56. In the Spanish tradition, as in many other countries, this term was by and large taken to mean a political regime opposed to monarchy. Given the popu-larity of constitutional monarchy in Spain, the term "republicanism" is still not well received by most ordinary people, as it evokes the Spanish Second Republic (1931–39) and the Civil War (1936–39).

57. The first term, *civismo*, is the only one that already exists in correct Spanish, but it connotes being civilized and having good manners rather than re-ferring to what Pettit had in mind in using "civicism". *Ciudadanismo* and *civici-smo* are both neologisms. The former was the most popularized in Spanish public debate, but I find it equivalent to "citizenism," which again does not adequately capture the meaning of "civicism." This is why I prefer *civicismo*. Zapatero and his colleagues in Nueva Vía used indiscriminately *civicismo* and *ciudadanismo*, or

their equivalents in other languages, such as *citoyennisme* in French (Rodríguez Zapatero 2004a).

58. One striking example of the latter was the regulation of the Spanish public broadcaster, RTVE. According to Pettit, "while the constitutional-democratic aspect of republicanism would require making this body independent of government, as indeed he had himself canvassed, he would find it very difficult to go ahead with the policy and that if he did, he would quickly come to resist the change, as he found himself under challenge from the newly independent station" (Pettit 2008c, 13). Spain has poorly developed cable television; and although there are actually two digital satellite platforms with several channels each, they are not widespread. The majority of people in the country only have access to between eight and ten TV channels, including three or four public ones, two of which are national and belong to RTVE, with the other being owned by the autonomous communities, by townships, and by private entities. To this scenario of scarce alternatives, we have to add that RTVE usually has the largest audience. Consequently, it is quite a powerful broadcaster in terms of capacity to disseminate information and to control the government.

59. It is noteworthy that Zapatero never tried to determine the content of this review, nor did he provide special information to Pettit. The two met again in June 2006, however, when Pettit was in Spain for a university lecture; they had a long, intense conversation in the Moncloa, where Zapatero continued to show interest in knowing more about civic republicanism. This conversation, like all their encounters, was reported in the Spanish press (see, for instance, *El Mundo* 2006, 9; Sen and Merino 2006, 14), and was featured in the weekly magazine *Tiempo* (Martín 2006). Pettit came back to Spain in 2008 to lecture in Sevilla, at the invitation of the Andalusian government (see, for instance, *Diario de Sevilla* 2008; *El Mundo* 2008a, 32; *El País* 2008, 12).

60. It is worth mentioning that, besides the review itself, Pettit was also included in an initiative of Zapatero's government to keep it in touch with philosophy and reflection: an international "Panel of Experts," or "Council of Sages," as it has been called, created in late 2007 to receive new advice from international progressive intellectuals to aid in designing his electoral program for the 2008 campaign. The panel gathered together fourteen distinguished intellectuals or leaders, including the Nobel Prize–winning American economist Joseph Stiglitz; the Australian antinuclear advocate and Nobel Laureate Helen Caldicott; the ex–senior vice-president of the World Bank and Professor of Economics in the London School of Economics Nicholas Stern; the President of the Foundation on Economic Trends and American economist Jeremy Rifkin; the University of California Professor of Linguistics George Lakoff; the Hans Kellog Professor of Government at Notre Dame University Guillermo O'Donnell; and Pettit himself (see, for instance, *El País* 2007 and *El Mundo* 2007, 18).

61. Pettit was present in the Spanish media on all these occasions, giving interviews to *El País*, *El Periódico*, *El Mundo*, and *La Voz Digital*, among others (see,

for instance, Sáenz-Díaz 2007). The content of the audit was explained by the Left in the media as well (see, for instance, Estefanía 2007; Elorza 2008).

62. This book had a strong influence in the determination of the ideological priorities in the PSOE, as proven by the "political report" presented by Jesús Caldera at the party's general conference in May 2008 (*El Mundo* 2008b).

63. For a general overview of the government in the light of its intended ideological innovation, see Kennedy (2007). The whole political term of any prime minister has plenty of right and wrong decisions, of thoughtful or more spontaneous statements, of inspired or unfortunate moves. A single decision generally means nothing. In order to assess the general performance of a particular prime minister it is necessary to review the majority of his actions and interventions, or at least the most substantial and significant ones, without getting unnecessarily caught up in the details. It is a matter of an overall macro judgment, rather than micro judgment. When we commonly say, for instance, that Ronald Reagan and Margaret Thatcher led libertarian or neoliberal governments, or even models of this political philosophy, we mean that the general set of their political initiatives could fall under this heading in an important way. We do not mean that all and any of their initiatives can be rated as indisputably libertarian or neoliberal. It is a generalization that we need for this kind of judgment.

64. The purpose of this chapter and the entire book is to make a judgment not about the person of Zapatero or his deep motivations, but about his *persona* and his government's *performance*. Again, what is relevant in the case of Reagan and Thatcher is not what they *really* thought or believed, or their *real* motivations to lead their countries as they did. We can leave this task to historians and biographers. What is relevant for us in assessing the philosophical allegiance of a political leader is what this leader actually *does*, as well as what he or she publicly *claims to do*. In other words, I want to show that civic republicanism played a role, at least officially, in Zapatero's public discourse.

65. See note 10.

66. The word *crispación* in Spanish is quite specific. It evokes tension and (self-restrained) outrage. Perhaps the closest equivalent is "high irritation." But while one can unwittingly irritate others, the Spanish verb *crispar* seems to include an active and voluntary element of provoking tensions. Some analysts opt for translating it as "rancor" (Gunther and Montero 2009, 137), but this seems closer to the idea of resentment, and although there could be some of it in the PP's politics of *crispación*, it is certainly not the core of its meaning. Following a suggestion made by Robert Fishman, I will use the expression "harshening" of political life.

67. Pettit's response to these two complaints raised by the PP can be found in the appendix to chapter 3.

68. Zapatero presented a detailed proposal to congress on May 13, 2005, after two years without any fatalities from terrorism in Spain. The text was passed with the approval of all the political parties, except the PP.

69. The PP claimed to have "talked" to ETA during the previous ceasefire in 1999, but not to have "negotiated" with it. Leaving aside these terminological niceties, Zapatero, in the opposition at that time, offered his support to Aznar's government in order to facilitate the peace, in contrast with Rajoy's lack of cooperation in 2005.

70. The Statute of Autonomy is the highest political legislation in an Autonomous Community and regulates its basic powers and institutions. As pointed out above, the Autonomous Communities are the regions into which Spain is divided, which already enjoy a considerable amount of political decentralization—close to, but not as much as the amount in federal states—, and have their own institutions such as a government and a parliament. See note 16. The Statute of Autonomy is roughly equivalent to each state's constitution in a federal state, although there are some important differences. The process for reforming a Statute of Autonomy begins and is mostly conducted in each Autonomous Community but, once adopted there, it ultimately needs to be approved by congress at the national level. For this reason the national government and the majority party in the congress are very important (see Gunther and Montero 2009, p. 45 and chap. 3).

71. The Spanish Constitutional Court still had made no decision about this issue at the time this book went to press.

72. The PP even encouraged those Spaniards who opposed this kind of decentralization to exercise their right of popular initiative to send the congress a bill in order to reverse these reforms.

73. In addition, in both cases, and although he may well have sincerely believed that he was pursuing normative principles, he could also have strategic reasons for doing what he did.

74. There have been other important initiatives during the term, such as the reform of the criminal code to prevent gender violence (December 2004); the basic law of education, which added a civic education course—involving the teaching of fundamental values as the human rights, the respect for minorities, and so on—to the required curriculum (May 2006); and the law for promoting equality between men and women (January 2007). For a fuller review see chapter 3. Considerations of space lead me to focus only on the three examples mentioned in the text.

75. There were very few countries in the world permitting it, and Spain never had been known for being ahead of other European countries on social issues like this. Zapatero could easily have argued that he did not have enough support to introduce this reform. There were no public demonstrations or any other form of popular pressure on behalf of the gay community in favor of marriage rights. The proposal did not even occupy a privileged place in public debate.

76. The Catholic Church has traditionally enjoyed in Spain a position of social dominance, increased during the Franco dictatorship by several legal and political privileges. Although nowadays it is not as central and powerful as it used to

be, it is still privileged in many ways. It is the only faith, for instance, to which taxpayers can give money via their annual tax returns, even though there around one million Muslims now in Spain as well as significant numbers of other faiths. Article 16 of the Spanish Constitution proclaims that "no confession shall have a state character" and then states that "the public authorities will take into account the religious beliefs of Spanish society and maintain the consequent relations of cooperation with the Catholic Church and other confessions." Jurists say the state's commitment to finance the church expired many years ago, that it is unconstitutional now, and that the church has failed to meet the commitment in Article 2.5 of the 1979 Concordat to "achieve by itself sufficient funds to meet its needs."

77. The conservative media were quickly up in arms. As happens in many other places, there was an active social movement in defense of the traditional family; some massive public demonstrations protesting against the government were even held. It is true, however, that the majority of the people favored this reform. According to the periodic barometer poll taken by the Centro de Investigaciones Sociológicas in June 2004, 66% of Spanish citizens were in favor of permitting same-sex marriage, while only 26% were opposed (CIS 2004).

78. The traditional European welfare state rests on three pillars: social security, which granted retirement pensions for workers; a public health care system for all, with free and universal access; and a public education system, at least for primary and secondary school, with free and universal access as well (see note 9).

79. During his first term, Zapatero recurred often to the idea of nondomination as a basic value. On several occasions he referred particularly to the group that, from his point of view, has suffered the most domination at all different times and places: women. See, for instance, what he said in this respect in an interview with *Le Monde* (Rodríguez Zapatero 2004a).

80. The Dependency Act established a system of progressive recognition of dependencies and conceived a process that could last several years; it started immediately with the hardest cases and provided them with care or assistance and a subsidiary economic compensation. This initiative has been widely criticized, however, because the development of both the recognition of dependencies and the supply of assistance or the concession of compensation has been much slower than planned, causing a great deal of dissatisfaction in Spanish society.

81. This was true even when the vast majority of the people backed this initiative in general (CIS 2006).

82. In his initial speech supporting the bill in congress, Zapatero declared: "With this Act, your honors, we create a new right of citizenship, a right of equal access to essential elements for the autonomous life of many people, to their dignity, a right whose significance for its subjects' lives is undeniable, since it is inherent to people's dignity and free development of personality.... Today I

feel particularly proud of belonging to a country which reinforces its genuine wealth: the dignity of and cohesive solidarity with its citizens" (Rodríguez Zapatero 2006, 11135).

83. This was the alleged reason, not the fear of other terrorist attacks by Al Qaeda, for withdrawing Spanish troops. On the other hand, it had been one of the central promises made by Zapatero during the election campaign and responded to a massive complaint of the Spanish people. As pointed out above, a majority of Spanish citizens disapproved of the war and fiercely opposed Spanish participation in it.

84. From the beginning it gained the strategic support of Turkey and twenty other countries, and is now backed by eighty different countries, including all the members of the G8 and most Islamic countries. The current high representative for the AoC is Jorge Sampaio, former president of Portugal, and the high-level group advising him is made up of several renowned personalities, such as Desmond Tutu, Mohammad Khatammi, and Federico Mayor Zaragoza. The project is an attempt to dispute Samuel P. Huntington's ideas about a clash of civilizations, promoting mutual understanding, joint actions, and bridges of communication (Huntington 1998).

85. See the Alliance of Civilizations website: http://www.unaoc.org/content/view/29/83/lang.english.

86. Some older precedents of republicanism buried in the rich Spanish humanist tradition were set very early on by the exceptional philosopher Ramon Llull (1232–1315), and were later championed by Bartolomé de las Casas (1474–1566), who developed a precursor to the idea of human rights; Juan Ginés de Sepúlveda (1490–1573); and Fernán Pérez de Oliva (1494–1533), whose *Diálogo por la Dignidad del Hombre* (1585) was a famous defense of free will as the basis of human dignity. A good later precedent can be found in the noteworthy Spanish baroque writer Baltasar Gracián (1601–58), and more concretely in his *El Héroe* (*The Hero*) (1637), a discussion of Macchiavelli's *Prince* (1513) criticizing his apparent abdication of public virtues, and advocating the possibility and desirability of a virtuous political leader. Nevertheless, and despite their influence in other respects, none of these precedents was directive in the formation of Spanish socialist thinking, which still stands as the clearest root of contemporary Spanish socialist republicanism.

87. While Iglesias (1850–1925) and Prieto (1883–1962) were more politically important for the PSOE—the former actually being the party's founder in 1879, and the latter Minister with Alcalá Zamora and Azaña during the Second Republic—Giner de los Ríos (1839–1915) and Besteiro (1870–1940) were those with higher education and with a more consolidated and influential program. Giner de los Ríos was educated in Barcelona and Granada, and was then law professor at the Complutense University of Madrid; he was also one of the founders of the Institución Libre de Enseñanza. Besteiro was educated in that same Institución Libre de Enseñanza and the Complutense University of Madrid, then

in the Sorbonne in Paris, and at several universities in Germany; he finally became philosophy professor of the Complutense University. Another Spanish influence explicitly acknowledged by the prime minister is the poet and philosopher María Zambrano, even though she did not belong to the Left tradition (de Toro 2007, 211). María Zambrano (1904–91) was a disciple of Ortega Gasset, exiled in various countries when Franco came to power. Among her works on political philosophy and democracy, *Horizontes del Liberalismo* (1930), *El Hombre y lo Divino* (1953), and *Persona y Democracia* (1959) are worth mentioning. Particularly important are her works dealing with literature and philosophy, like *Filosofía y Poesía* (1940), *La Agonía de Europa* (1945), or *La Tumba de Antigona* (1967).

88. And he adds: "And for attaining that goal, that no one feels dominated, we have to start with freedom, with the freedom of thinking differently from others, and the freedom of these others to dispute your ideas, your power, and your authority. This is the most fertile, the richest, and the most creative" (de Toro 2007, 210–11).

89. Considering what they understood as freedom, they might well fall under the umbrella of civic republicanism. Republicanism differs from liberalism in its particular understanding of freedom—freedom as nondomination. But things were not so clear in the 1920s and 1930s, when every defense of freedom seemed to be necessarily related to liberalism (see chapter 2 for the evolution of both doctrines). The label "liberal" has been dominant throughout the whole nineteenth century and part of the twentieth and has often been used to refer to very different values and doctrines. Indeed, some of the champions of republicanism, such as Immanuel Kant, John Stuart Mill, and the American Founding Fathers were for a long time considered as liberals. Leaving aside names and labels, the important thing is that what these early Spanish socialists were advocating is what nowadays can be described as a civic republican understanding of freedom.

90. This adjective refers to the German philosopher Karl Christian Friedrich Krause (1781–1832), who was quite influential in Spain at that time, after being introduced by Julián Sanz del Río, the Institución Libre de Enseñanza, and Francisco Giner de los Ríos. Krause himself was not a particularly interesting thinker, but his influence in Spain gave Spanish intellectuals the opportunity to access other German scholars or essayists such as Bernstein, who were very much more interesting.

91. Posada, for instance, distinguished the social person from the individual, and advocated a social orientation for the state in granting equality as well as freedom, highlighting political liberties, the value of tolerance, and political decentralization. He criticized liberalism as well as Marxism and anarchism. For a thorough account of his vast body of work, see Laporta (1974).

92. The opposition between the radical and the moderate conceptions of Spanish socialism was politically represented by the different ideologies and contrasting styles of two of the leaders of the PSOE during the Civil War: on the one hand, Indalecio Prieto, much closer to the centrist and republican (but not socialist)

Presidents Niceto Alcalá Zamora and Manuel Azaña, and on the other, President Francisco Largo Caballero, closer to the communist party and to several anarchist factions. For an excellent recent description of the Second Republic and the Civil War, which includes an account of this contrast, see Beevor (2006), and also Preston (2007).

93. Good examples of this are Vallespín (2001), Béjar (2001), Giner (2004), and Camps (2004). Of course, some of them also criticized some of the ambiguities or silences in Zapatero's official political position, such as Ovejero and Gargarella (2001), Taibo (2007), and Ovejero (2007). But their general stance was one of a public defense of some version of civic republicanism.

94. Delgado-Gal is a journalist, writer, and editor of the prestigious monthly journal *Revista de Libros*.

95. Once again, remember that the term "liberalism" means different things in Europe and the United States, as well as in the academy (see note 4).

96. See de Francisco (2001) and Ovejero and Martí (2002). Delgado-Gal reacted to these responses in Delgado-Gal (2002), and again two years later in Delgado-Gal (2004).

97. See, for instance, Genovés (2004), Sánchez Cámara (2004), Lassalle (2007), more than twenty-five articles by Luis María Anson in *El Mundo*, *La Razón*, and the digital newspaper *El Imparcial*, and especially three long articles by Pedro J. Ramírez (2006a,b; 2007).

98. See Delgado-Gal (2001) and Genovés (2004). This accusation concerned Pettit from the beginning, and was one of the first things he challenged before continuing his review of Zapatero's policies (Pettit 2008c, 13).

99. See Delgado-Gal (2001), Genovés (2004), Sánchez Cámara (2004), and Ramírez (2007). There are continuing philosophical debates between liberal and republican theory, of course, many of which rehearse similar themes; see, for example, Laborde and Maynor (2007). A principal issue is whether republicanism affords a truly original and different understanding of liberty, and, if so, whether this is philosophically appropriate.

100. See Delgado-Gal (2001) and Lassalle (2007). The most aggressive, sometimes offensive pieces are in del Pozo (2007, 2008) and Anson (2008b). Many of the assaults were outrageously false, at times bordering on the absurd. Perhaps the most striking case of this kind of *ad hominem* arguments in the Spanish press, combined with a sort of reiterative obsession with Pettit, is offered by Luis María Anson, the founder and former editor in chief of the conservative newspaper *La Razón*, and president of the digital newspaper *El Imparcial*, as well as a regular contributor to *El Mundo*. Anson mentioned Pettit in more than 25 articles in several media outlets, rarely with criticisms of his doctrine or reviews of the Spanish government. See, for instance, Anson (2008a,b). There is no interest in reviewing such articles, except to reiterate that Anson promulgated a number of falsehoods: for example, that Pettit was in permanent and direct contact with Zapatero, that he was inciting or urging all of Zapatero's decisions, or that he had proposed

eliminating education in Spanish in Catalonia. These and other statements motivated Pettit to refute them in a public letter in *El Imparcial* (Pettit 2008b). This article, in turn, received a response by Anson (2008c). The attacks from the Right were redoubled once Pettit presented his civic audit to Zapatero's government in June 2007 in Madrid, and quadrupled with the publication of the book *Examen a Zapatero* in December of that year. Pettit's audit was quite positive and some on the Right may have judged it essential to defuse its effect by targeting its author.

101. The publication of this article was apparently the reason why the Vodafone Foundation withdrew its organization of Philip Pettit's scheduled presentation of his audit in Madrid only a couple of weeks beforehand. Presumably they were not interested in a conflict with *El Mundo* and Pedro J. Ramírez. The organization of the presentation was undertaken instead by the Complutense University Foundation and the Centro de Estudios Constitucionales y Políticos.

CHAPTER 2
CIVIC REPUBLICAN THEORY

1. There are some complexities that I ignore. Does intimidation rely on the possession of an arbitrary power of interference, for example, when these others intimidate me on the basis of an illusion? Yes, strictly: my lack of information gives them power; indeed it would do so, even if they too were lacking in the required information. But doesn't such intimidation amount, then, to active deception and manipulation? Not strictly. It might occur on the basis of deception but it only requires the failure to provide information, whether that be an instance of the active withholding of information or not.

CHAPTER 3
THE THEORY IN PRACTICE? SPAIN 2004–8

1. But with help from Philipp Koralus, who provided research assistance, and with an unfailing supply of information and advice from a number of friends who helped me along the way. I should mention above all José Luis Martí, who was tireless in answering some very tiresome questions; David Casassas, who provided me with a personal assessment of the Zapatero government; and Amalia Amaya Navarro, who gave me some invaluable advice on legal matters. Tori McGeer offered detailed and constructive comments on the revision of the text.

2. See http://www.elpais.com/articulo/sociedad/Cabrera/presenta/borrador/asi gnatura/Educacion/Ciudadania/sera/evaluable/elpporsoc/20060606elpep usoc_6/Tes.

3. Crime statistics are notoriously difficult. Thus, whereas Hooper (2006, 344), reports that there were 100 offenses per 1,000 population in 2001, the

government claims that in 2007 this figure was just 50 per 1,000 (Government of Spain 2007, 14). It is hard to believe that there could have been such a precipitous fall in six years; it is more likely that different statistics are being used.

4. The other components in the index relate to the functioning of government in reacting to democratic opinion, political participation, and political culture.

5. The only part of the constitution that rings ominously to an outside ear is Section 8.1. This requires the armed forces of Spain "to defend its territorial integrity and the constitutional order," without making clear who is to pass judgment as to whether that integrity or order is under challenge. The danger of that clause was illustrated by the ominous message in 2006 from the then head of the Land Forces in Spain that the army might be required to intervene, if the proposed new Statute of Autonomy for Catalonia was not watered down—as indeed it eventually was, in the normal democratic process. Did Lieutenant-General Aguado assert a presumptive right on the part of the armed forces—or even his supreme commander, the King—to intervene in the democratic process? He may not have been taken seriously in a democracy like Spain. But the question remains as to whether the Spanish Constitution supported that assertion. If it did, then surely the Constitution ought to be amended on this point.

CHAPTER 4
AN INTERVIEW WITH PRIME MINISTER ZAPATERO

1. Translator's note: The concept "liberal" means nonconservative right wing in Spain, and in Europe in general, almost the opposite of what it means in the United States.

2. Translator's note: The CIS is the Centro de Investigaciones Sociológicas, the Center for Sociological Research, a public but apparently independent institution. Their polls are generally reliable.

3. Translator's note: The Consejo General del Poder Judicial (CGPJ) is the body of administration of the judiciary in Spain. It is not hierarchically superior to any court, since judges are completely independent, but it has the power to discipline those judges who break the law.

CHAPTER 5
GIVING PHILOSOPHY A PUBLIC LIFE

1. For the content of the memo and criticism of it, including mention of this response, see http://www.counterpunch.org/summers.html.

2. When he emphasizes the public role of a shared conception of justice in a well-ordered society, the later Rawls (1993) suggests that something more abstract than the two principles would serve as a shared ideal. But even at that point

he seems to suggest that, if things go as they ought to do, the shared conception of justice will assume concrete form in something close to his two principles.

3. Nozick can be seen as someone who equates freedom with noninterference but then argues, not that noninterference should be promoted by the state, but that like any other agent the state should be required to exemplify it. That would make the state an impossibility but for his argument in support of the ultraminimal arrangement.

4. In the first model, to adapt John Rawls's (1971) terminology, the appeal of universal freedom as nondomination is an instance of the appeal of the right; under the second it is an instance of the appeal of the (commonly recognized) good.

5. Thomas Nagel (1989, 119) argues that people may overcome limited altruism when "contribution to an impersonal good becomes a personal motive for their occupants." This is precisely what is envisaged within the economy of esteem. See Brennan and Pettit (2004) on the "intangible hand," as distinct from the "invisible hand."

6. Left-of-center liberals, as noted in chapter 2, will seek to deal with this problem, not by revising the view of freedom as noninterference, but by insisting that such freedom is not the only value to be promoted.

7. In a series of recent lectures, Amartya Sen has been criticizing philosophies that fail this desideratum as transcendental theories. See http://www.news .harvard.edu/gazette/2007/05.24/01-sen.html. See too Sen (2009), which was unavailable at the time of writing.

8. This is objectionable but not in a way that casts doubt on Ronald Dworkin's use of the "envy test." Dworkin invokes envy, not in the psychological sense that makes it into an attitude it is hard to avow, but rather in the technical sense of an attitude one agent, A, has toward another, B, whenever A prefers B's holdings to A's own. See Dworkin (2002, 117).

References

Anson, L. M. 2008a. El reto de Zapatero: La relación con la Iglesia. *El Mundo*, March 28.

———. 2008b. Examen a Zapatero. *El Mundo*, January 22.

———. 2008c. Respuesta a Philip Pettit. *El Imparcial*, February 14.

Barbería, J. L. 2004. El armazón del cambio. *El País*, March 21.

Beevor, A. 2006. *The battle for Spain: The Spanish Civil War 1936–1939*. London: Penguin.

Béjar, H. 2001. Todos somos republicanos. *El Mundo*, December 13.

Bellamy, R. 2007. *Political constitutionalism: A republican defense of the constitutionality of democracy*. Cambridge: Cambridge University Press.

Bentham, J. 1843. *Anarchical fallacies*. Vol. 2 of *The works of Jeremy Bentham*, ed. J. Bowring. Edinburgh: W. Tait.

Berlin, I. 1958. *Two concepts of liberty*. Oxford: Oxford University Press.

Bernstein, E. 1909. *Evolutionary socialism*, trans. E. C. Haley. London: Independent Labour Party.

Besson, S., and J. L. Martí. 2008. *Legal republicanism*. Oxford: Oxford University Press.

Blair, T. 1998. *The Third Way: New politics for the new century*. London: Fabian Society.

Bodin, J. 1992. *On sovereignty*. Cambridge: Cambridge University Press.

Bohman, J. 2007. *Democracy across borders: From demos to demoi*. Cambridge, MA: MIT Press.

Boix, C. 1998. *Political parties, growth and equality. Conservative social democratic economic strategies in the world economy*. Cambridge: Cambridge University Press.

Bourdeau, V., and R. Merrill, eds. 2007. *La republique et ses démons: Essais de républicanisme appliqué*. Maison-Alfort, France: Editions Ere.

Braithwaite, J. 1997. On speaking softly and carrying big sticks: Neglected dimensions of a republican separation of powers. *University of Toronto Law Journal* 47:305–61.

Braithwaite, J., and P. Pettit. 1990. *Not just deserts: A republican theory of criminal justice*. Oxford: Oxford University Press.

Brennan, G., and J. Buchanan. 1981. The normative purpose of economic "science": Rediscovery of an eighteenth century method. *International Review of Law and Economics* 1:155–66.

Brennan, G., and A. Hamlin. 1995. Economizing on virtue. *Constitutional Political Economy* 6:35–36.

Brennan, G., and P. Pettit. 2004. *The economy of esteem: An essay on civil and political society.* Oxford: Oxford University Press.

———. 2005. The feasibility issue. In *Handbook of analytical philosophy*, ed. F. Jackson and M. Smith, 258–79. Oxford: Oxford University Press.

Brugger, W. 1999. *Republican theory in political thought: Virtuous or virtual.* New York: Macmillan.

Campillo, O. 2004. *Zapatero. Presidente a la primera.* Madrid: La Esfera de los Libros.

Camps, V. 2004. La libertad republicana. *La Vanguardia*, August 4.

Celso, A. N. 2006. Spain's dual security dilemma: Strategic challenges of Basque and Islamist terror during the Aznar and Zapatero eras. *Mediterranean Quarterly* 17(4):121–41.

Chislett, W. 2004–9. Inside Spain. Real Instituto Elcano, http://www.realinstit utoelcano.org/wps/portal/rielcano_eng/Insidespain.

———. 2008. *Going places: Spain.* Madrid: Telefonica.

CIS. 2004. Barómetro Junio. Centro de Investigaciones Sociológicas, http:// www.cis.es/cis/opencm/EN/1_encuestas/estudio/ver.jsp?&estudio=3994&_ element=head.

———. 2006. Barómetro Mayo. Centro de Investigaciones Sociológicas, http:// www.cis.es/cis/opencm/EN/1_encuestas/estudios/ver.jsp?&estudio=5657&__ element=head.

Consejo General. 2004. *Informe sobre la situación de los órganos judiciales. Año 2003.* Madrid: Consejo General del Poder Judicial.

Crick, B. 1997. Still missing a public philosophy? *Political Quarterly* 68(4): 344–51.

de Francisco, A. 2001. Quién teme al republicanismo? *El País*, December 6.

de Toro, S. 2007. *Madera de Zapatero. Retrato de un presidente.* Barcelona: RBA.

del Pozo, R. 2007. Sobresaliente. *El Mundo*, June 23.

———. 2008. Examen del filósofo. *El Mundo*, January 18.

Delgado-Gal, Á. 2001. Republicanismo: El conejo en la chistera. *El País*, November 26.

———. 2002. Sobre Pettit y otras brumas. *El País*, February 27.

———. 2004. El republicanismo y el PSOE. *Cuadernos de Pensamiento Político*, October 4.

Diario de Sevilla. 2008. España ha funcianado bien no sólo gracias a Zapatero. March 14.

Dworkin, R. 2002. Sovereign virtue revisited. *Ethics* 113:116–43.

———. 2006. *Is democracy possible here? Principles for a new political debate.* Princeton, NJ: Princeton University Press.

El Mundo. 2006. June 6.

———. 2007. November 14.

———. 2008a. Pettit: Es malo para la democracia gobernar indefinidamente. March 14.

———. 2008b. Vuelve Philip Pettit. May 13.

El País. 2007. November 14.

———. 2008. El gran reto de Zapatero será su relación con la Iglesia. March 15.

Elorza, A. 2008. Libros en campaña. *El País*, March 1.

Esping-Andersen, G. 1990. *The three worlds of welfare capitalism.* Princeton, NJ: Princeton University Press.

Estefanía, J. 2007. Auditoría cívica al Gobierno socialista 1 y 2. *El País*, June 24 and 25.

Estlund, D. 2009. Utopophobia. Manuscript.

Ferguson, A. 1767. *An essay on the history of civil society.* Edinburgh: Millar and Caddel. Repr. New York: Garland, 1971.

Fink, Z. S. 1962. *The classical republicans: An essay in the recovery of a pattern of thought in seventeenth century England.* Evanston, IL: Northwestern University Press.

Fishman, R. 2007a. On being a Weberian (after Spain's 11–14 March): Notes on the continuing relevance of the methodological perspective proposed by Weber. In *Max Weber's "Objectivity" Reconsidered*, ed. L. McFalls, 26–89. Toronto: University of Toronto Press.

———. 2007b. On the significance of public protest: Puzzles and challenges of Spanish politics. *Newsletter of Iberian Politics* 2(1):1–9.

Frey, B. 1997. *Not just for the money: An economic theory of personal motivation.* Cheltenham, UK: Edward Elgar.

Frey, B., and R. Jegen. 2001. Motivation crowding theory: A survey. *Journal of Economic Surveys* 15:589–611.

Gamper, D. 2004. Philip Pettit: El poder de la ciudadania. *La Vanguardia*, August 4.

García Agustín, O. 2006. Republicanismo y el nuevo socialismo español de Rodríguez Zapatero. *Sociedad y Discurso 9*.

Genovés, F. 2004. Zapatero y su musa filosófica. *Libertad Digital*, July 23.

Giddens, A. 1994. *Beyond Left and Right. The future of radical politics.* Cambridge, UK: Polity Press.

———. 1998. *The Third Way. The renewal of social democracy.* Cambridge, UK: Polity Press.

Giner, S. 2004. Sendas republicanas. *El País*, April 3.

Government of Spain. 2007. *Tres años de gobierno Abril 2004–7.* Madrid: Ministerio de la Presidencia.

Grabosky, P. N. 1995. Counterproductive regulation. *International Journal of the Sociology of Law* 23:347–69.

Gunther, R., and J. R. Montero. 2009. *The politics of Spain*. Cambridge: Cambridge University Press.

Hall, S. 1998. Nowhere man. *Sunday Times*, October 18.

Honohan, I. 2002. *Civic republicanism*. London: Routledge.

Honohan, I., and J. Jennings, eds. 2006. *Republicanism in theory and practice*. London: Routledge.

Hooper, J. 2006. *The new Spaniards*. London: Penguin Books.

Huntington, S. P. 1998. *The clash of civilizations*. New York: Simon and Schuster.

Kaiser, D. 2007. A letter on rape in prisons. *New York Review of Books* 54:22.

Kekic, L. 2007. The Economist Intelligence Unit's Index of Democracy. http://www.economist.com/media/pdf/DEMOCRACY_INDEX_2007_v3.pdf.

Kennedy, P. 2007. Phoenix from the ashes: The PSOE government under Rodríguez Zapatero 2004–2007: A new model for social democracy? *International Journal for Iberian Politics* 20(3):187–206.

Kriegel, B. 1995. *The state and the rule of law*, trans. M. A. LePain and J. C. Cohen. Princeton, NJ: Princeton University Press.

Laborde, C. 2008. *Critical republicanism: The hijab controversy and political philosophy*. Oxford: Oxford University Press.

Laborde, C., and J. Maynor, eds. 2007. *Republicanism and Political Theory*. Oxford: Blackwell.

Laporta, F. 1974. *Adolfo Posada: Política y sociología en la crisis del liberalismo español*. Madrid: Edicusa.

Lassalle, J. M. 2007. Desmontando a Pettit. *ABC*, June 21.

Long, D. C. 1977. *Bentham on liberty*. Toronto: University of Toronto Press.

Lovett, F., and P. Pettit. 2009. Neo-republicanism: A normative and institutional research program. *Annual Review of Political Science* 12:11–29.

Lovett, F. N. 2001. Domination: A preliminary analysis. *Monist* 84:98–112.

———. Forthcoming. *A general theory of domination and justice*. Oxford: Oxford University Press.

Madison, J., A. Hamilton, and J. Jay. 1987. *The federalist papers*. Harmondsworth, UK: Penguin.

Magone, J. M. 2004. *Contemporary Spanish politics*. London: Routledge.

Majone, G. 1993. The European Community between social policy and social regulation. *Journal of Common Market Studies* 31.

Mandeville, B. 1731. *Free thoughts on religion, the church and national happiness*. London.

Maravall, J. M. 1982. *The transition to democracy in Spain*. New York: St. Martin's Press.

Margalit, A. 1996. *The decent society*. Cambridge, MA: Harvard University Press.

Martí, J. L. 2006. *La república deliberativa*. Madrid: Marcial Pons.

Martí Font, J. M. 2004. Entrevista a Philip Pettit: Zapatero me invita a que examine su Gobierno dentro de tres años. *El País*, July 25.

Martín, C. 2006. El maestro Pettit examina al alumno Zapatero. *Tiempo*, June 5–11, 36–38.

Maynor, J. 2003. *Republicanism in the modern world.* Cambridge, UK: Polity Press.

McCubbins, M. D., and T. Schwartz. 1984. Congressional oversight overlooked: Police patrols vs fire alarms. *American Journal of Political Science* 28: 165–79.

Nagel, T. 1989. What makes a political theory utopian? *Social Research* 56: 903–20.

Navarro, N. 2004. Entrevista a Philip Pettit: La democracia puede caer en la dictadura electoral. *El Periódico*, October 28.

Nozick, R. 1974. *Anarchy, state, and utopia.* Oxford: Blackwell.

O'Neill, O. 1987. Abstraction, idealization and ideology in ethics. In *Moral philosophy and contemporary problems,* ed. J.D.G.Evans. New York: Cambridge University Press.

OECD. 2004. Education at a glance. http://www.oecd.org/document/34/0,2340,en_2649_34515_35289570_1_1_1_1,00.html.

Oldfield, A. 1990. *Citizenship and community: Civic republicanism and the modern world.* London: Routledge.

Ortega y Gasset, J. 2003. Invertebrate Spain (1922). In *Modern Spain: A documentary history,* ed. J. Cowans. Philadelphia: University of Pennsylvania Press.

Ovejero, F. 2007. Es de izquierdas la politica del PSOE? *El Noticiero de las Ideas,* July 31.

Ovejero, F., and R. Gargarella. 2001. Renovación ideológica o de qué se habla que me apunto? *El País*, May 21.

Ovejero, F., and J. L. Martí. 2002. No sólo de Pettit vive el republicanismo. *El País*, January 4.

Paley, W. 1825. *The principles of moral and political philosophy.* Vol. 4 of *Collected works.* London: C. and J. Rivington.

Papell, A. 2008. *Zapatero 2004–2008: La legislatura de la crispación.* Madrid: Foca.

Parfit, D. 2000. Equality or priority? In *The ideal of equality,* ed. M. Clayton and A. Williams, 81–125. New York: St Martin's Press.

Pateman, C. 1988. *The sexual contract.* Oxford, UK: Polity Press.

Pérez Díaz, V. 1993. *The return of civil society: The emergence of democratic Spain.* Cambridge, MA: Harvard University Press.

Pettit, P. 1996. Freedom and antipower. *Ethics* 106: 576–604.

———. 1997. *Republicanism. A theory of freedom and government.* Oxford: Oxford University Press.

———. 1999. *Republicanismo,* trans. Antonio Domenech. Barcelona: Paidos.

Pettit, P. 2001. *A theory of freedom: From the psychology to the politics of agency.* Cambridge, UK: Polity Press/New York: Oxford University Press.

———. 2002. Keeping republican freedom simple: On a difference with Quentin Skinner. *Political Theory* 30:339–56.

———. 2005. The domination complaint. *Nomos* 86:87–117.

———. 2006. Freedom in the market. *Politics, Philosophy and Economics* 5: 31–49.

———. 2008a. The basic liberties. In *Essays on H.L.A. Hart,* ed. M. Kramer. Oxford: Oxford University Press.

———. 2008b. Carta a El Imparcial. *El Imparcial,* February 14.

———. 2008c. *Examen a Zapatero,* trans. J. L. Martí. Madrid: Temas de Hoy.

———. 2008d. Freedom and probability: A comment on Goodin and Jackson. *Philosophy and Public Affairs* 36:206–20.

———. 2008e. *Made with words: Hobbes on language, mind and politics.* Princeton, NJ: Princeton University Press.

———. 2008f. Republican liberty: Three axioms, four theorems. In *Republicanism and political theory*, ed. C. Laborde and J. Manor. Oxford: Blackwells.

———. 2009a. Legitimate international institutions: A neorepublican perspective. In *The philosophy of international law*, ed. S. Besson and J. Tasioulas. Oxford: Oxford University Press.

———. 2009b. Varieties of public representation. In *Representation and popular rule*, ed. Ian Shapiro, Susan Stokes, and E. J. Wood. Cambridge: Cambridge University Press.

———. Forthcoming. A republican law of peoples. In Republicanism and international relations, special issue, *European Journal of Political Theory* 9.

Pocock, J. 1975. *The Machiavellian moment: Florentine political theory and the Atlantic republican tradition.* Princeton, NJ: Princeton University Press.

Prego, V. 2001. Entrevista a José Luis Rodríguez Zapatero: Yo soy quien marca mis tiempos. *El Mundo,* July 8.

Preston, P. 2007. *The Spanish Civil War: Reaction, revolution and revenge.* London: Norton and Co.

Priestley, J. 1993. *Political writings.* Cambridge: Cambridge University Press.

Ramírez, P. J. 2006a. ¿Zapatero contra Pettit? *El Mundo,* January 9.

———. 2006b. Zapatero ya toca el piano. *El Mundo,* January 15.

———. 2007. Informe a Philip Pettit sobre el estado del puente de Tacoma. *El Mundo,* June 3.

Raventós, D. 2007. *Basic income: The material conditions of freedom.* London: Pluto Press.

Rawls, J. 1955. Two concepts of rules. *Philosophical Review* 64:3–32.

———. 1971. *A theory of justice.* Oxford: Oxford University Press.

———. 1993. *Political liberalism.* New York: Columbia University Press.

———. 1999. *The law of peoples.* Cambridge, MA: Harvard University Press.

————. 2001. *Justice as fairness: A restatement*. Cambridge, MA: Harvard University Press.

Richardson, H. 2002. *Democratic autonomy*. New York: Oxford University Press.

Robbins, C. 1959. *The eighteenth century commonwealthman*. Cambridge, MA: Harvard University Press.

Rodríguez Zapatero, J. L. 2000. Speech to the PSOE after being elected as secretary general of the party. PSOE, http://www.psoe.es.

————. 2004a. Entretien a M. Zapatero: Pour M. Zapatero, l'Espagne est revenue a l'élan européen. *Le Monde*, July 29.

————. 2004b. Nomination (or Investiture) Debate, 1st. Session, April 8, Congress of Deputies. Congress of Deputies Records, no. 2 http://www.congreso.es.

————. 2004c. Nomination (or Investiture) Debate, 3rd. Session, April 15, Congress of Deputies. Congress of Deputies Records no. 2, http://www.congreso.es.

————. 2004d. Nomination (or Investiture) Debate, 4th. Session, April 16, Congress of Deputies. Congress of Deputies Records no. 3, http://www.congreso.es

————. 2005. Speech in the debate for the approval of the reform of the civil code, June 30, Congress of Deputies. Congress of Deputies Records no. 103, http://www.congreso.es.

————. 2006. Speech in the debate for the approval of the Dependency Act, November 30, Congress of Deputies. Congress of Deputies Records no. 219, http://www.congreso.es.

Ruiz Ruiz, R. 2006. *La tradicion republicana*. Madrid: Dykinson.

Sáenz-Díaz, M. 2007. Entrevista con Philip Pettit. *El Periódico*, June 22.

Sánchez, I. 2002. Los pensadores de Zapatero. *El siglo de Europa,* 528.

Sánchez Cámara, I. 2004. Ciudadanismo y socialismo. *ABC*, July 28.

Sanchis-Moreno, F. 2007. Access to Justice in Spain under the Aarhus Convention. Asociacio para la Justicia Ambiental, http://www.elaw.org/assets/pdf/es.aj2.spain.2007.pdf.

Sandel, M. 1996. *Democracy's discontent: America in search of a public philosophy*. Cambridge, MA: Harvard University Press.

Schumpeter, J. 1942. *Capitalism, socialism and democracy*. New York: Harper.

Sellers, M.N.S. 1995. *American republicanism: Roman ideology in the United States Constitution*. New York: New York University Press.

Sen, A. 1985. *Commodities and Capabilities*. Amsterdam: North-Holland.

Sen, A. 2009. *The Idea of Justice*. Cambridge, Mass.: Harvard University Press.

Sen, C., and J. C. Merino. 2006. Zapatero pasa la auditoría de Pettit. *La Vanguardia*, June 6.

Sevilla, J. 2002. *De nuevo socialismo*. Barcelona: Crítica.

Skinner, Q. 1984. The idea of negative liberty. In *Philosophy in History*, ed. R. Rorty, J. B. Schneewind, and Q. Skinner. Cambridge: Cambridge University Press.

Skinner, Q. 1985. The paradoxes of political liberty. In *The Tanner Lectures on Human Values*, ed. S. McMurrin, 227–50. Cambridge: Cambridge University Press.

——. 1990a. Pre-humanist origins of republican ideas. In *Machiavelli and republicanism*, ed. G. Bock, Q. Skinner, and M. Viroli. Cambridge: Cambridge University Press.

——. 1990b. The republican ideal of political liberty. In *Machiavelli and Republicanism*, ed. G. Bock, Q. Skinner, and M. Viroli. Cambridge: Cambridge University Press.

——. 1998. *Liberty before liberalism*. Cambridge: Cambridge University Press.

——. 2008. *Hobbes and republican liberty*. Cambridge: Cambridge University Press.

Slaughter, S. 2005. *Liberty beyond neo-liberalism: A republican critique of liberal government in a globalising age*. London: Macmillan Palgrave.

Spitz, J.-F. 1995. *La liberté politique*. Paris: Presses Universitaires de France.

Spitz, J. F. 2005. *Le moment républicain en France*. Paris: Gallimard.

Taibo, C. 2007. Zapatero, en la izquierda? *La Vanguardia*, June 21.

Temple, M. 2000. New Labour's Third Way: Pragmatism and governance. *British Journal of Politics and International Relations* 2(3).

Tonkin, B. 1998. Why New Labour is in search of an ideology. *The Independent*. April 25.

Torres Mora, J. A. 2008. Personal communication.

Treglown, J. 2009. "Grave-digging." *Granta* 105, spring.

Trenchard, J., and T. Gordon. 1971. *Cato's letters*. New York: Da Capo.

Tribunal Supremo. 2007. STS 888/2007, de 25 de octubre.

Vallespín, F. 2000a. La izquierda posible. *El País*, July 23.

——. 2000b. Socialismo posideológico. *El País*, May 5.

——. 2001. El "socialismo cívico." *El País*, July 21.

Van Dijk, J. 2005. The Burden of Crime in the EU: Research Report for European Crime and Safety Survey (ICS). http://www.gallup-europe.be/euics/Xz38/downloads/EUICS%20-%20The%20Burden%20of%20Crime%20in%20the%20EU.pdf.

Van Gelderen, M., and Q. Skinner. 2002. *Republicanism: A shared European heritage*, 2 vols. Cambridge: Cambridge University Press.

Van Parijs, P. 1995. *Real freedom for all*. Oxford: Oxford University Press.

Vincent, A. 1998. New ideologies for old? *Political Quarterly* 69(1).

Viroli, M. 2002. *Republicanism*. New York: Hill and Wang.

Weinstock, D., and C. Nadeau, eds. 2004. *Republicanism: History, theory and practice*. London: Frank Cass.

White, S., and D. Leighton, eds. 2008. *Building a citizen society: The emerging politics of republican democracy*. London: Lawrence and Wishart.

INDEX

Acebes, Miguel Ángel, 14
Africa, 71, 105, 127
Alianza Popular (Popular Alliance),
  163n11. *See also* Partido Popular
Alliance of Civilizations (AoC), 22–23, 71,
  105, 127, 176n84
Almunia, José, 165n15
Althusser, Louis, 110
Andalusia, 165n16
Anson, Luis María, 178n100
AoC. *See* Alliance of Civilizations
Arendt, Hannah, 111, 121
Aristotle, 137
armed forces, 180n5
Arteta, Aurelio, 26
Autonomous Communities: and control
  of public power, 88–89; culture and
  education in, 97–98; defined, 165n16;
  establishment of, 115; power of, 20,
  88–89; PSOE and, 165n16; and Spanish
  unity, 20, 89–90, 95–100, 95–97; Statutes of Autonomy in, 174n70; Zapatero
  on, 115–16
autonomy, individual, 154–55, 158
Azcárate, Gumersindo de, 25
Aznar, José María, 4–5, 7, 14, 19, 22,
  163n11

balkanization of Spain, Autonomous Com-
  munities and, 20, 89–90, 95–97
Béjar, Helena, 26
benevolent despotism, 42, 44–45, 108, 152
Bentham, Jeremy, 43, 45–46, 50, 67
Berlin, Isaiah, 28, 142, 155; "Two Con-
  cepts of Liberty," 45
Bernstein, Eduard, 25

Besteiro, Julián, 24, 25, 176n87
Blair, Tony, 2, 8–9, 12, 22, 109–10
Blanco, José, 165n17
Bodin, Jean, 42
Bono, José, 5, 165n17, 165n18
Borrell, José, 164n15
Britain, 40–41, 105
Brugger, W., 53
Buñuel, Luis, 25
Bush, George W., 5, 22, 171n53

Caldera, Jesús, 165n17
Caldicott, Helen, 172n60
Camps, Victoria, 26
Cassassas, David, 26
Catalan Socialist Party, 20
Catalonia, 88–90, 97–98, 180n5
Catholic Church: Partido Popular and,
  5; same-sex marriage opposed by, 21,
  123; state in relation to, 84–85, 93,
  174n76
Cato's Letters (Trenchard and Gordon),
  141
Center for Intelligence against Organized
  Crime, 82
Centro de Investigaciones Sociológicas
  (CIS), 113, 180n2
Cervantes, Miguel de, 111
CGPJ. *See* Consejo General del Poder
  Judicial
Chacón, Carme, 165n17
change, 6, 165n18
checks and balances, 40, 60, 65, 114
Chislett, William, 91
church-state relations, 84–85
Cicero, 40, 67

disadvantaged, empowerment of, 54–56, 78–81
Doménech, Antoni, 26
domination, 33–34; familiarity with, 148; without interference, 2–3; private and public, 3, 18, 34, 48; in Roman tradition, 3, 34; wage slavery as, 47. *See also* civic control over state domination; nondomination
dominium/dominus, 3, 34, 48, 52, 72
Dworkin, Ronald, 181n8

economy: globalization and, 130–31; and nondomination, 75–76; Spanish, 5, 14, 75–76, 132. *See also* neoliberalism
education, 77, 97–98, 120–21, 132
egalitarianism, 152
electoral system, 163n12
elitism, 137
energy, 78
environment, 78
equality: of citizens in politics, 59–62, 65; freedom and, 3, 13, 40–41, 72–73; Law of Equality, 79, 80, 122, 123; limitations of, as political ideal, 153, 155; republicanism and, 40
ETA. *See* Euskadi Ta Askatasuna
ethics, public, 123
European Union: Spain's entry to, 4; Spain's role in, 71, 106, 126–28; and Spanish governance, 89; Spanish unity and, 96–97
Euskadi Ta Askatasuna (ETA; Basque Homeland and Freedom): aims of, 113; González and, 4; history of, 163n10; Madrid terrorist attack blamed on, 14–15; prison conditions for, 83, 101–2; Zapatero and discussions with, 19–20, 82–83, 93, 100–101
exit options, 55–56
eyeball test, 3, 17–18, 79

factional ideals. *See* sectional ideals
FAES. *See* Fundación para el Análisis y los Estudios Sociales
feminism, 47–48
Ferguson, Adam, 66

Fernández, Matilde, 5, 165n17, 165n18
Fernández de la Vega, María Teresa, 10, 165n18
Fink, Zera, 31
Florence, 40
foreign policy, 22–23, 70–71, 105–6, 126–29. *See also* international relations
Fraga, Manuel, 163n11
freedom: civic republicanism and, 2–3, 16–18, 32–40, 72–74, 140–42; decline of republican concept of, 42–46; democracy and, 13–14; equality as element in, 3, 13, 40–41, 72–73; feminism and, 47–48; liberalism and, 43–46; negative, 142; negative concept of, 28, 32, 45, 48; as nondomination, 2–3, 16–18, 32, 34–40, 43–45, 72–74, 106–8, 111, 140–42; as noninterference, 2–3, 34–39, 43–46, 48, 74, 106–8, 111, 140–42, 152–53; as participation in sovereign self-rule, 31–32; as primary good, 140–41; republicanism and, 34, 38–42, 47–48; socialism and, 13, 24–25, 46–48, 112; Spanish people and, 113; state role in, 3, 18; Zapatero and, 3, 6–7, 11, 13–14, 111–12
French Revolution, 41
Friedman, Milton, 8
Fundación para el Análisis y los Estudios Sociales (FAES; Foundation for Analysis and Social Studies), 5, 164n13

García Lorca, Federico, 25
gay marriage, 21–22, 79, 122–23
gender violence, 79, 122–23
Gibraltar, 105
Giddens, Anthony, 9
Giner, Salvador, 26, 111
Giner de los Ríos, Francisco, 24, 176n87, 177n90
Ginés de Sepúlveda, Juan, 176n86
globalization, 130–31
González, Felipe, 4, 6, 10, 19, 109–10, 162n7, 166n21
good mood or disposition (*talante*), 7, 115
Gordon, Thomas, *Cato's Letters* (with John Trenchard), 141